Safety Sucks!

The Bull $H!# in the Safety Profession They Don't Tell You About.

Samuel Goodman

ISBN 978-0-578-68436-9

Published and distributed by Hominum, LLC

Dedication

I want to dedicate this book to the light of my life Avery and the love of my life Jerel – thank you both for always loving and believing in me. And to my mother Geneva "Mommoo" Goodman and late father Harold "Poppy" Goodman – thank you for being the most supportive and loving parents anyone could ask for.

I want to thank the amazing mentors I have had in my career: Jim Rice, Steve Fuller, and Donnie Pena – thank you for showing me the way.

I want to also dedicate this to those that have spent their entire careers fighting tirelessly in a broken system to just make things better.

Table of Contents

Preface

Hello, howdy, and hi! Welcome and thank you. I hope that you find this book interesting, the stories inside entertaining, that you find the content to be valuable, and that you walk away with some ideas on how we can *Make the World a Better Place to Work*.

Change is hard, I get it. But, we move beyond bad ideas by introducing better ideas. I truly believe that by continuing to have these "hard" conversations in an upfront, honest and fun way, we cultivate betterment. The safety profession has been stagnant for far too long. Safety folks are abused and misused, they're often underpaid and overworked, they are undervalued and not appreciated, they find themselves being blamed and shamed when accidents occur, they are torn between the frontline and management, they have been forced to knowingly promote flawed, ineffective and disproven safety management systems – to preach from a bible in which they do not believe, and we just can't seem to grasp why a) we can't find quality safety people b) we hemorrhage good safety professionals to other professions and organizations c) safety practitioners are rendered ineffective d) safety people are left burned out and frustrated.

I am not complaining, I am being honest. How's that old saying go? "The first step to fixing a problem is admitting that you have a problem." There's a lot of truth in that – I guess that's how new sayings become old sayings. Let's face it, we've not been very honest with ourselves. We have stuck our heads in the sand and not faced the flaws of our profession. It is time for a strong dose of truth and honesty. But I have learned the hard way that being upfront, honest and fun, tends to get you categorized as brash. So, I find myself in trouble quite a bit; I guess I am a little polarizing – who would have thought? So, before we go any further, I want to state what this book is not.

It is not meant to bash the safety profession. I really love what I do, I really love our profession, and I really love all my "safety family" out there. I do not believe in "eating our own," but I do believe in calling out the bull shit that exists in and around our job. People shouldn't be miserable at work, period. We shouldn't force amazing (world changing) safety professionals to flee this job due to the mental and emotional toll our positions are currently structured to inflict. We get better, not only by calling out the bull shit, but by doing something to make it better.

It is not meant to drive people away from the safety profession, god knows we need good safety people. If you have ever had the task of trying to fill a safety position, you know that the struggle is real. As much as jobs within our profession continue to grow, our applicant pool seems to remain the same size (or shrink). I hope that this book gives people that are thinking of pursuing "safety as a career" some insights into the "sucks" of our profession. Additionally, and more importantly, I hope that it challenges each of us to do better, that it challenges companies, professional organizations, and institutes of higher education to re-evaluate the education, care, and feeding of safety professionals.

I am not aiming this at a particular person, company, or organization, I'm aiming at all of them. We must do better – all of us. I nearly left this profession due to many of the stories in this book; I've had very close friends leave. Amazing safety professionals, just like that, poof! Gone! We share the responsibility of making things right. We share the responsibility to make things better. We owe it to those just starting in this wacky job, we owe it to those that have spent their entire careers fighting tirelessly in a broken system to make things better, and we owe it to ourselves – those that are currently working the job with no chance of retirement in sight (my retirement estimates say that I'll get to retire around age 115).

Back to me not complaining, there's another old saying "if you bring me a problem – bring me a fix." I plan on doing that; I'll offer some ideas for bettering the things that

I rant about. But I think it's also a good idea to state that I'm not a guru; I do not hold all the answers and I'll never try to convince you that I do. Look, I am not big on labels. But if I leave a void, folks will label me for themselves. So, if you want to call me anything, I guess I am more of an evangelist – an evangelist of betterment. I am simply a zealous advocate of making things better. I think the best way of doing that is through conversations. We start down the path of betterment by putting the not-so-great stuff out in the open and talking about it. Dissenting voices drive us towards betterment – they water and fertilize the soil in which betterment grows. I'm simply plowing the field, planting the seeds, watering, and fertilizing. You get to decide what you do with the yield.

At the end of the day, I hope that you walk away from this experience with some ideas of things you want to change and some ideas on how you're going to change them. I hope that it inspires you to seek out the "suck" that is in the safety profession and to do something about it. Hell, I hope you don't limit it to the safety profession. Every job has "suck" that should be dealt with. So I hope that you become a betterment evangelist in your areas of influence – a zealous advocate for making thing better. With that being said, I encourage you to share this book! Pass it around, send your friends a copy, photocopy one of the wonky stories and share it in a meeting, or leave a community copy in the office. I hope that it acts as a catalyst, as a conversation starter, as an opportunity to talk about making things better.

Thank you for joining me on the mission of Making the World a Better Place to Work (for safety people too)!

Introduction

Let me start by saying that I love my profession! I know that's probably not the dramatic and angry introduction that you were expecting; but I really do love my job. I feel that I'm doing what I was born to do, I've found my life's work – pretty cheesy, right? But really, I've found my life's professional purpose. It's such an amazing feeling to wake up in the morning and know that what you are doing for a living matters. Like really matters, like you are – helping to make people's lives better – kind of "matters." That's a complete one hundred and eighty degree turn from where I was early on in my career. To completely level with you, I nearly left the profession outright. I had literally boxed up my office and had drafted my letter of resignation. My manager at the time, who is a mentor and an amazing friend, talked me down from the ledge. But, from that day on I knew that something had to change. I was frustrated, burned-out, I was pissed off and I felt lied to. I remember asking myself: "Did I just waste the first few years of my professional life on something that I now hated and didn't believe in?" "Am I stuck in this stupid job forever?" Those are some pretty soul crushing thoughts. We will explore how I got there in a moment. We'll expand on the "sucks" that lead to me plotting my escape as we meander through the book. But before I dive too deep, let me tell you about who I am.

Let's start in a time before safety in strange and mystical far away land – Richlands, Virginia. Richlands is a small town in rural Virginia; south western Virginia if you're into splitting hairs. In Richlands, coal is king, and Jesus Christ is a close second. I grew up running around in the woods, hunting, camping, playing music, skateboarding, and riding "four-wheelers" (quads for my friends outside of the southeast portion of the United States). I was a punk rock country art creative kind of kid, that's a thing, right? I'd listen to The Misfits, play bluegrass guitar, shoot a deer, and go to a mural painting class – all in the same day. From elementary to high school and on to college, I was never a phenomenal student; I mostly just squeaked by with C's and the occasional D. I'd rather be playing music or drawing. I mostly found school boring and unfulfilling. Due to this, I found myself in trouble from time to time with teachers and other authority figures. When I say trouble, I don't mean the juvenile detention system kind of trouble. Think more like "punk kid with a smart mouth" type of trouble. Most of the trouble that I found myself in during these early years had very little to do with actual trouble and a lot to do with one very upsetting question to the gatekeepers of small-town status quo: "Why?" I love the small town I grew up in, but let's be totally honest – small towns aren't really known for their open mindedness; they don't really appreciate dissent or those that go against the grain. They do not really embrace free-thought or free-speech. They typically embody the "that's the way we've always done it" mentality. A 14 year old punk kid challenging teachers on the usefulness of their curriculum, asking town preachers "are you sure god exists – like really sure? Because it all seems kind of made up to me." Does not go over all that well. Little did I know that this "trouble" would be one of my biggest blessings upon entering the professional world and a massive part of what kept me in the safety profession – challenging things that don't make sense, being a dissenting voice, and finding a better way is now my passion.

Upon graduation from High School I entered college and started studying Administration of Justice. I had dreams of entering law enforcement or continuing on to study law. It's funny, as I reflect now, my father mentioned to me that I should think about going into safety as I was enrolling in college. I remember asking him at the time "what the heck is safety?" and thinking to myself "god that sounds bland and boring!" You see, dad had retired from the mines and later (after being bored to death with retirement) returned to work in the commercial nuclear space. He spent the later portion of his life traveling around and working outages during the spring and fall. He knew the value of safety and could see the growing career opportunities in the space. But I was young, I wanted action, and more importantly, I wanted to carry a gun, so I quickly enrolled in my first Administration of Justice classes and got started. This dream lasted until I discovered the fire service; the alure of the action was enticing. The satisfaction of helping my neighbors and community pushed it over the top. I ran away from college and became a firefighter and EMT. I loved it, hell I still do! How can you not? Everyone is a nerd for the lights, sirens and big red trucks. I'll gladly admit that I still turn into a little kid when I hear that Federal Q-Siren wind up. Sadly, dad passed away around this time in my life. I was awfully close with my father; he was my best friend and biggest supporter. When he died, I floated around aimlessly for a bit. I needed a change and I needed to get the hell out of that small town. I followed in his footsteps and started working outages in nuclear power plants. I took any jobs I could find to get my foot in the door. I worked as a laborer, as a helper, and eventually worked my way into coatings and a few other specialties. During this experience I developed a love for power generation. This is also when I was first exposed to safety as a profession; I finally got see what dad was talking about. I decided then and there that I was going into safety. It was the opportunity to take a deeply rooted desire to help people and couple it with my newly discovered love of working in power generation. To find out how to get into safety, I sought out safety people. Fortunately, I was blessed to find some amazing mentors early on. These mentors guided me into the profession and I still lean on them for their advice and friendship today.

So, after some classes and mentoring, I found myself In my first safety position. I was hired as a "Safety Tech I" for a large contractor in the power generation space (they only gave me "1" because there was nothing lower). At this point, I had only been in the power generation space for a couple of years. So, I started in the safety profession at a pretty young age. I like to say that "I grew up in safety." As I mentioned, I started and spent a sizable portion of my career in commercial nuclear generation. From my first position as a safety tech, I took a position as a safety specialist I; working my way from a specialist I to a specialist IV. From there, I became a manager, I moved on to fossil generation, construction, maintenance, and various other safety management and leadership roles for large-scale contractors and utilities. I spent many years traveling from project to project all across the United States. That travel eventually brought me to Phoenix, Arizona on a temporary assignment, one that (10 years later) I'm now comfortable calling a permanent assignment.

In 2019 I started The HOP Nerd Podcast and I founded HOP University in 2020; both sharing the same mission of "Making the World a Better Place to Work." I now have the opportunity to work with organizations all over the globe as they evolve towards Human & Organizational Performance and doing safety differently, I get to interview thought leaders and influencers in the safety space every single week, and I get to have amazing conversations with brilliant and amazing safety people and industry leaders every day. Sounds like a blast, huh? Well, it almost didn't happen.

Within my first few years as a safety professional, I was looking for a way out. I was done! But why? "Sam, I thought you said you loved it, I thought you said it was your life's work, yada, yada, yada..." Yeah, it is now, but not so much then. At the time I was tired, I was worn out, and I craved a life outside of work. I was burned-out, I was done with the beatings and I was tired of being the scapegoat for company failings. I was exhausted from constantly fighting to make things better in a broken system and from being placed in a position of being at odds with management and frontline employees. My first few years in safety probably taught me the most, I learned amazing and important life lessons during my early professional years. But I was left disenfranchised with traditional safety and management approaches. I was angry from being forced to knowingly promote flawed, ineffective and disproven safety management systems and ideas – from being forced to preach from a bible in which I did not believe. I was simply over it and ready to move on.

So, where does this big long rant lead? I wish I knew about the "sucks" of safety; I wish someone would have told me. Not so I could avoid the profession, but so I could be prepared for the profession. I'm a firm believer in the old saying "you can either do this job or you can't." It takes a very unique person to make a well-rounded safety professional. This is evermore true as we move beyond the simplistic traditional approaches of yesterday – but more on that, experience, and training later.

Many amazing safety professionals enter this field blind to what awaits them. Sadly, many do not survive and leave to pursue careers in other fields. Amazing safety professional, professionals that we desperately need, folks that would and should be doing amazing things in this space, hemorrhaged to other professions. I was almost one of them. So, when I get the questions "What do I need to do to get into safety?" or "Do you have any advice for a young safety professional?" Questions that I get several times every week. I always take the time to first share the "suck;" the stuff that I wish someone would have told me – the stuff someone should have told me. One of the very first things I like to share with them is this: they'll have days where they'll think "I can't believe they pay me to do this!" But that they'll have just as many days where they will think "you could never pay me enough to do this!" I like to share the not-so-great stuff right out of the gate. I want them to know that it's not sunshine, lollipops, and cotton candy. I share with them the gritty and honest truth. I'm not trying to scare them off, I'm not I promise! I really want them to be prepared for what they will be facing as they enter this field. We've not done a very good job of that in my opinion. Institutes of higher learning teach compliance this and regulatory that, workshops and training courses just teach more of the same, and it seems that we as individual professionals would just rather not talk about it. Nothing to see here! Everything is fine! This is how we've always done it! "Pretty please come fill our open safety position? Everything is great here!" That leads to some of my "why" for writing this book. I'll admit, some of it is out of laziness. Rather than having to answer these questions every week, I can have them read this book instead. But most of my "why" is to inspire people to join me in challenging and changing the not-so-great things that are a part of this profession. We deserve better and so do future safety professionals.

If you have been around safety for more than a moment, you'll probably relate to a lot of this. These stories and situations will sound eerily familiar. That's a very interesting part of this, its not contained to a single company or industry – this bull shit is systemic. If you're new to the profession, don't let this scare you off. Read these stories, learn from them, and think about how you can counter the "suck." Whether you are new or old, I hope that the "suck" pisses you off as much as it does me. This is our profession and we must change it, we must raise the bar, and we must do better. We must stop accepting mediocrity and "but that's the way we have always done it" as acceptable answers. We must be the dissenting voice, we must challenge and call bull shit when we see bull shit! Together we can make the world a better place to work. But it takes all of us. I hope that you find this book funny and enjoyable. But ultimately, I hope that it inspires you to challenge the status quo and bull shit that surrounds the safety profession. We share the responsibility to make things better – to right the ship. We owe it to those just starting in this wacky job, we owe it to those that have spent their entire careers fighting tirelessly in a broken system to make things better, and we owe it to ourselves –

17

those that are currently working the job with no chance of retirement in sight.   With all of that out of the way, let's get down to the afore mentioned "Suck!"

You'll never know...

Have you poured your heart and soul into an assignment and not even received an honorable mention? Have you ever worked 90 hours a week trying to support an understaffed project to only get the "side-eye" for leaving a few minutes early on a Friday? Have you been blamed after an event happened? Did you knock something out of the park to only have someone else receive credit for your blood, sweat and tears? Welcome to the safety profession. It really is a thankless career. To top that, you will never really know your successes. You'll never know how many lives that you have improved, the people that you have inspired, the amount of betterment that you have created, the number of poor outcomes you prevented or minimized, or the induvial and organizational growth you've caused. But one thing is for certain, you will hear about anything that you do not execute perfectly on.

Here is a cold-hard fact: A lot of companies hold safety practitioners culpable for the failings of the organization, the failings of flawed safety management systems and approaches, and the failings of poor leaders.

Post-accident, everyone knows the most logical question is to ask, "where was safety at when this happened?" or to demand that they manage down the classification of an injury. If safety had only been there; they could have swooped in and prevented the bad thing from happening with their magical safety powers. Did you lob off an employee's arm? No worries! Just call your local safety pro and demand that they case manage it out of being a recordable injury. If they can't, you can just blame it on them! "If we just had a better safety person…" I hope the sarcasm came across loud and clear in that.

I was working a contract safety position supporting a large-scale construction project in the southern states. This was a big one, a lot of dangerous work and a lot of people. You are probably familiar with the type; jobsite trailers as far as the eye could see. There was a variety of contractors supporting this client, all just trying to get their respective jobs done. Everything was going surprisingly well, so well that the site was planning a cookout. When managers are grilling hotdogs and hamburgers, you know things are going extremely well or layoffs are near. One day towards the end of the project and a few days after the "1 bazillon hours since someone messed up" cookout, an employee walking into the location tripped and fell over thin air. The result? Your run of the mill sprained ankle. That sucks, right? At this point the "green" safety folks are thinking to themselves "where the hell is he going with this? An ankle sprain? Big deal!" (and I totally agree with you by the way). My seasoned safety pros out there already know how this story goes; they've heard or seen it a thousand times. The employee was rushed to the site nurse and the injured ankle was quickly tended to. After a few hours of ice and resting, the ankle was only swelling more, and someone finally decided to get this employee the care they needed. All that sounds pretty normal so far, huh? Well, you will see how quickly things change. The safety person 'responsible' for the employee was urgently summoned to the site clinic to escort this employee to a local hospital. They weren't summoned to be helpful; they were not called to care for the employee or look out for their wellbeing. Their mission: Ensure "conservative but adequate care" at the hospital. This is also known as "pretty please doctor, don't treat beyond first aid?" Well things didn't go as planned. The employee ended up in an ankle boot and prescribed some pain medication. The safety person returned to site with their head down and tail tucked between their legs. They were blamed and scolded by their own company and the client; they were placed on unpaid administrative leave and several days later they were fired for "failing to meet the minimums outlined in their job description." Basically, they failed to manage the case. To summarize, an employee received correct and adequate care that they desperately needed and deserved for an injury that they incurred while performing work for the company, so we fired the safety person. Yeah, it is as stupid as it sounds and that's why it's at the top of this bull shit list.

I remember being in shock after watching this unfold. I vividly remember my thoughts "This can't be real life, right? Some ones pranking us." Unfortunately, this was very much real. Sadly, I have seen a similar story playout several times. Let's just state this fact right now: Safety isn't responsible for safety. As safety professionals, we often find ourselves being held accountable for things that are not ours. We are forced to bear crosses that aren't ours to bear. Why? a) It's easy and people are lazy: Busy (lazy) managers and leaders simply do not have time to keep their people from getting hurt. They most certainly don't have time to waste on "doing the safety persons job!" You know, like making sure that injured employee from their crew is being cared for, learning how an event transpired, or fixing problems. "Hey safety!" is a much easier answer. b) safety is a good scapegoat: At this point, it's already been established that the accident was mostly the safety persons fault anyways (ugh, if they had only been there! ugh, if only they were a better case manager!). It only makes sense that safety should be responsible for fixing it, right? How many corrective actions have you owned, written, implemented, and closed that shouldn't have been yours to own? Management and leaders "own" safety when things are going well; but it's the safety departments baby when things go awry. It's easy to say "We" were successful, but when things go wrong, it quickly becomes "You" failed. I don't want to really take a dive into the responsibilities of safety professionals, but look, here's the deal. Throughout industry, we continue to (incorrectly) view safety as an outcome. If the outcome is not-so-great, we must assign blame! Gee thanks traditional safety! Who better to assign said blame to than the person that literally has "safety" in their title? Safety does safety, so safety should be responsible for safety, right? Hitting a little too close to home? We are just getting started.

Here is another cold-hard fact: Safety professionals are held to a different standard. I spent some time at a large power plant on the east coast; it was quite an interesting gig. The job? Work Monday through Friday, 10 hours each day, providing safety support for a couple of crews installing security upgrades around a plant. Translation: be the safety guy for several crews installing massive bundles of razor wire on top of existing massive bundles of razor wire. Sounds like the stuff nightmares are made of, right? Believe it or not, no major injuries happened. These folks were absolutely amazing at what they did. But this isn't a story of safety success – this is a horror story. Late one Thursday evening I was frantically summoned to the site director's office. I remember the conversation as if it were yesterday. "So, I've been getting reports that you safety people have been leaving early. It's fraud to claim hours that you didn't actually work!" as I started to speak, he quick cut me off "Don't say anything, I'm going to pull the gate logs in the morning. I'm excited to fire all of you!" I finally got a word in "Sir, that's perfectly fine. But when you pull those logs, you need to be prepared to pay all of us for the hours that we are here and don't claim on our timecards." He glared at me; I could see him plotting in his head on how to dispose of my body after he strangled me. "I'll bet my job that you will not find a single safety person that doesn't exceed their daily hours. We all work more hours than we record – the crews need coverage and you refuse to pay overtime so...." He quickly cut me off "I'll take that bet!" needless to say, I kept my job, but I never got my payout for all of those unclaimed hours. In this job, you are often wrong even when you are right.

A few years later, I took over the safety department on a small production site down south. On paper, it seemed like a dream job. It was a small site, the pay was decent, the job had regular hours, the site had two additional safety techs, and it was about a 30-minute drive to the beach. Epic, right? Well, a few weeks into the job and I had the full picture. The sites culture had been destroyed by previous management regimes. People despised management, they hated the safety department, they were untrusting, they were angry, and they had every right to be. The company was numbers driven; using "sticks & carrots" to drive down incident rates. They favored the stick more than the carrot, the previous leadership (term applied loosely) team had weaponized the safety department. They would audit, beat, fire, and repeat. They had historically been the henchmen for the location's manager. Close your eyes and imagine everything you could possibly do to harm organizational culture. Yep, that is exactly what they did.

24

So, after some tweaking and tuning on the site's safety team, we set our sights on change. I'll leave out the nitty gritty details, that's another book for another day. Let's just say that It was hard. This was one of the hardest times in my career. I remember feeling down and out; I felt like my actions were doing nothing. I was drowning and help was not coming. I would leave work already dreading the drive back the following morning. It was depressing and I was ready to pack up and leave. One warm spring day I was outside, dipping (chewing smokeless tobacco for my non-rednecks out there – it was a bad habit and yes I've quite since then), cussing god, and drafting my resignation letter in my head, when one of the frontline workers came over to chat. "Who pissed in your cheerios?" He said. "Eh, just one of those days, you know how it goes!" I had just spent 2 hours in a meeting arguing with a manager to not fire an employee over a hand injury they had reported – I had just seen the employee carrying their things out the gate; I guess my frustration was showing. What he said next changed my life completely; it totally changed how I viewed my success as a safety practitioner: "Keep doing whatever you're doing, it's working." It honestly caught me off-guard. Stumbling in my reply "Wh- wha – what do you mean?" he looked at me like I had two heads and said "Did you not hear what I said? Things are getting better around here. I don't know how to describe it, but things just feel different. They feel different in a good way." He then muttered "You're not too bad to be a safety guy and all." Then we high-fived, hugged it out, it was super cool.

Ok, I made up that last bit. But that is what it felt like; that is what played out in my head. It was one of those "ah-ha" moments in my career. I left that location a little later down the road; I was pursuing career growth and had a good opportunity in another state. When I left, I left proud and with my head held high. Thing's weren't perfect by the time I left, but they weren't firing people for hand injuries anymore. I knew that I had left things better than I found them. Better is better, and better should be the only goal.

I want to challenge you individually to change how you think about your personal successes as a safety practitioner. You see, I thought success would be this big dramatic breakthrough. I thought that it would be me standing on a podium, victorious and overlooking my kingdom of positive change. Well, not exactly, but kind of. But that's not what success looks like. Success for us simply means making things better. That's it! To define success we need to go back to that primary mission we talked about earlier. Success simply equals Making the World a Better Place to Work – period. It's usually not big and sweeping changes; it usually happens very slowly over time. Piece by piece, step by step, it all adds up over the course of a career. Success, for us at least, is "You know… you're not too bad to be a safety guy and all." Keep the mission simple: Set out every day to just make the world a better place to work.

Safety professionals should not be excluded from that. We need to make the world a better place for us to work as well. But, a lot of the the problem remains. You will be held to impossible-to-meet standards. You'll never know how much great stuff your actions yielded; but you'll always know the bad. Even if that bad isn't your bad. You will be the scapegoat for shitty leaders and managers; you will be blamed when bad things happen. You will get grilled and questioned "where were you at when this happened?" "How much time do you spend in the field, anyways?" You'll be wrong, even when you're right. And all of that must change. How? We need to call bull shit when we see bull shit. We need to stop "falling on our swords" and accepting blame when bad things happen. We need to stop picking up the slack for terrible leaders; let them fail. We need to push back, we need to challenge, and we must drive the change we want to see. If you can't do that, you need to get the hell out of this profession. The rest of us have work to do.

The old mindsets around the safety profession are still pretty prevalent; but I see some positive change. There are a lot of great companies out there that have started to focus on the "care and feeding" of safety professionals. Some companies are evolving away from the traditional safety management styles that have left countless safety professionals frustrated, adopting more people-based approaches. All of which is leading to a lot of positive change in the profession. But we need to keep pushing, we need to stop enabling poor approaches and quit babying poor leaders. We need to demand that safety is integrated as part of the team, not just an external somebody to blame.

Until we make the world a better place to work for safety professionals, we'll keep losing great people and we will have to keep filling safety roles with anyone that will volunteer to take the beatings. But hey, at least you'll get some shitty conferences out of the gig.

Safety! FIX IT!

Let's just admit this fact right now, "Safety! Fix It!" Is the norm – "Safety! Fix It!" is bullshit. If it says "safety" or remotely even sounds like it's safety related, guess what? You get it. Enjoy! Go forth and fix the world! As a young safety professional, oh how you'll try! You will try and try before you realize that you are doing everyone else's job for them and you are actually making things much worse. The "Safety! Fix It! mindset has become deeply engrained in organizations; many believing that "safety is responsible for safety." Why would we be called "safety professionals" if our jobs were not to take care of safety so others do not have to worry with such things? (I really, really hope my sarcasm is translating well). A lot of companies promote, or even demand that these flawed beliefs manifest within their ranks. We are not off the hook either, some safety professionals promote or perpetuate the same of similar beliefs. Some by demanding control: "Call me before you do X, Y, or Z, so I can look at it before you start. My highly trained eye can see things yours cannot!" Or, by requiring that they themselves lead certain meetings or handle certain tasks; tasks so important that only a safety person should do them! Things like using a multi-gas meter to check a confined space or signing-off on a lock out / tag out, doing nothing other than growing dependence on the practitioner. A lot of us have promoted this flawed mindset at some point in our careers, but usually by mistake.

We all start "young and dumb;" we are all "green" at the beginning of our careers. Everyone, no matter what they end up doing for a living, they start as green as new grass. The problem is that we think that we are not; "I'm not like the others! I will not succumb to the same issues that my predecessors have!" When we first start in this job, we have visions of changing the world; visions that are often well founded (we'll get to that in a moment). We think to ourselves "I can do this better!" "I see all of the problems and know exactly what to do." "I have better ideas than those other foolish safety people!" "Why do they not just fix things?! I'm going to finally just fix things and they will see how it's done!"

Hopefully, if you are new to safety or just starting down this path, this book ends up being eye-opening. I hope that it opens your eyes to the battles that safety practitioners fight on a regular basis. Honestly, a portion of the intent of this book is to allow new practitioners to learn here, in a safe space, and with the opportunity to learn "the easy way." Learning the easy way rather than learning the way most of us did; the hard way. I'm speaking directly to my new safety people here: You need to understand that there are many great safety practitioners out there; good people just trying to make things better in a broken system. You will be required to learn this lesson in your career. So please learn this lesson now; learn this lesson the easy way rather than the hard way. None of it is as easy as it looks. I'm going to say that again; none of it is as easy as it looks. Amazing people have been in the trenches fighting for betterment over the span of their careers. Do not be so naive as to think that they simply chose to not make things better, that they are lazy, uncaring, or unknowledgeable. Many of these practitioners have pulled organizations and industries from the dark ages. I will promise you this, you will meet horrible safety people in your career. Some will be downright awful; you will meet people that should be nowhere near this profession. These people usually cause more harm than good. You are probably already familiar with the type, shiny safety cop badge and a baton, know-it-alls with big egos, and the like. These people become easier and easier to spot the longer that you do this job. But, as you spend some time in this field, you will quickly realize that there are many more amazing people than bad. As you gain experience, you will begin to understand the struggles and challenges that our safety family faces out there. The poor attitudes, the political landscapes, the old mindsets, and flawed traditional safety approaches that these people battle against every day. You will quickly come to realize that, while there is still a lot to change, they have actually created massive amounts of betterment. So please, always remember, it's not as easy as it looks. Especially if you are trying to change the world.

For my seasoned people reading this, I promise that I am almost done with the rookies. But please read on, I believe there are some pearls of wisdom in here for you as well and, you are next. There is nothing wrong with wanting to change the world. Hell, our motto around here is "Making the World a Better Place to Work." It would be pretty hypocritical if I insisted that that's only for me to do, huh? So, embrace your desire to change the world, do not lose that desire to create betterment, and be that relentless person that never stops trying to accomplish that mission. But take a little time to get to know the landscape, take a few moments to wrap your head around the problems, learn how to approach the issues from those that understand, and then jump into the battle. If you do not, you risk relentlessly pursuing the wrong things or trying to fix things in the wrong ways. You end up creating or perpetuating "Safety! Fix It!" Listen, your ideas, especially from those that did not grow up in these bull shit traditional safety management systems, are direly needed. Your fresh perspectives, your innovative approaches to tackling issues; we desperately need you. But, you will never change the world or tackle real issues if you are bogged down in managing portable toilet placement, spending your time inspecting fall protection equipment, re-hanging barrier tape, or being placed in charge of the amount of chairs in the break room. If you give in to the perceived ease and glory of "Safety! Fix It!" you will not have the time or the energy to Make the World a Better Place to Work. For my seasoned people out there (saying "old" usually gets me in trouble), you must do a better job of supporting those that are new to our profession. Do not apply the thinking that you consistently challenge; sticking to "that's the way we have always done it!" Give those new to this field your respect, your mentorship, your guidance, and your support. Do not ignore what they have to say or dismiss their ideas. It is on us to show them the lessons that we have learned. It's also on us to learn from them; to listen and take their thoughts and ideas seriously.

I realize that we went down the path of growing and cultivating new safety professionals. That was partially on purpose and partially because it is a topic that I will rant on any time that I am given the chance. I rant about it because we suck at it. I feel like we needed to address it because it is a significant portion of where the "safety! fix it!" mindset comes from. Circling back to the "young and dumb" portion of our careers, we often embrace the "Safety! Fix It!" model when we first start in the field, we then eventually awaken to the fact that we are being used and abused. Unfortunately, it does not stop. We simply go from being painfully unaware, to painfully aware. We have dug a hole in which we cannot get out of. If you challenge this now established model, you will be labeled: "The safety person doesn't care!" "The safety person said that it's not their job!" Mangers will quickly get involved;

33

usually outlining how it is your job and how "safety is responsible for safety!" Not fun stuff, huh? Yeah, they didn't tell me about that before I started either. Even if we already understand that "Safety! Fix It!" is stupid as we begin working for an organization, we often find ourselves dealing with mindsets and beliefs established by the company or our predecessors. Our predecessors more than likely did not create this maliciously, but by the time they realized what they had done it was simply too late. No one told them that it was wrong; that it would not lead to anything good. The organizations told them that it was what they wanted, and they were given what they wanted. I remember my first safety job well; I was basically 1-800-CALL-SAM-TO-FIX-YOUR-PROBLEMS. Wow, that's a long phone number, but you get what I am saying. Of course managers and leaders love this, how could they not? They get a safety person and a FIN (Fix It Now) team; two for one deal! "Oh, there is a barrier tape down?" Safety Sam to the rescue! "What? There is no toilet paper in the bathroom!?" with one fell swoop Safety Sam fixed the problem! How did I end up doing this? Simply put, I thought it was what I was supposed to do. I wanted to do a good job! I did not have the benefit of much of what we have already talked about. I knew my stuff, I knew the regulations, I knew the rules, I was pretty knowledgeable if I do say so myself. But I completely lacked "street smarts," I lacked wisdom, and I lacked the understanding of practical application. My job was to help, and I thought by fixing things that I was helping. I needed a mentor to guide me down a better path. So that's why I wanted to touch on that piece first and foremost. We need safety practitioners to start off on the right foot; to set the tone and to understand what their job actually is. They need to be mentored and taught better ways to fix things. Look, we could go on and on about the negative side effects of the "Safety! Fix It!" mindset. But, this is what I really want to say about it. If we as safety professionals, are constantly going out and fixing things, propping up things, and piecing stuff together, our organizations are not learning. Looking down on the work, leaders and managers see only that things went well, they see that there is toilet paper in the bathroom, and that that barrier tape looks damn good! In essence, we are just covering up problems. So, in addition to working ourselves into the ground, running all over our locations putting out fires and fixing problems, we are actually just hiding the fact that the problems ever existed. It's an endless cycle; it is a snowball really. A problem rears its ugly head, we put on our cape and rush out and fix the immediate issue, but we do not really fix the problem. It is repeated and it grows because we never actually learned; we never actually fixed anything other than a symptom. Hell, why would we need to learn? Isn't that the safety person's job too?

So yes, safety fam, we have to work on this too. We should not just point at the organization saying "Gahhh! Those meanies!" That obviously is not true and will not accomplish very much. We need to a) focus on starting professionals off on the right foot. We can accomplish a lot of this through much of what we just dove into. We need to start with the right mindset in the organizations in which we work. We must shape that mind set right out of the gate. If we do not, it will be shaped for us, and you will find yourself being the owner of a brand new shiny safety FIN team. We must firm up our beliefs as current practitioners and we must educate our upcoming people. b) We need to strongly challenge old and established "Safety! Fix It!" mindsets. We need to get vocal and refuse to be the "clean up" crew; refuse to act as the FIN team for our organizations. We might have started off on the wrong foot, but there is no excuse to perpetuate this flawed and dependent ideology. We must stop it dead in its tracks; viciously challenging it when it springs up. Let's get real, that will happen via pretty uncomfortable conversations; uncomfortable conversations that you must get pretty comfortable with having. You might be required to challenge some pretty high-ranking people in your companies and some of these conversations could potentially even get you fired. So just be aware of the dangers, I never claimed that Making the World a Better Place to Work would be easy. I also never said that this was for the faint of heart. Let me add this in here so I am not misunderstood: It is perfectly O.K. and encouraged to dive in and help someone in need or to help your company during challenging times. If someone has their hands full and they are asking for help, I am going to help them. If John Doe leader is being run ragged, I am going to help

36

him. That's not "Safety! Fix It!", that's just called being a good and caring person. Please understand that there is a difference. c) This one is a little more sensitive of a topic, ditching the not-so-great safety professionals out there. We have already established that they exist; there are "shit heads" out there and the live amongst us. There are also people that are not "shit heads," that just do not have the right mindset. If we have safety people who are shit heads, or those that simply refuse to take off the badge and lay down the baton, or folks that cannot hang up their capes, then maybe they should explore other career paths or professional opportunities. We will get into a little deeper detail on what type of person it takes to do this job a little later. But, we need to have this conversation. I am an absolute "people person;" I live for relationships. That is one thing that really drew me to this profession; the ability to really get to know people. That, coupled with helping people, making their working lives better, and my deep curiosity as to how things work. So, I take no pleasure in this portion of the conversation; this is hard to talk about for me. But, I feel that it is necessary. There are a lot of other great jobs these people can do in our organizations; I am by no means advocating that we throw them out on the street. For some, maybe that is the right answer. Shit heads, in particular. But for most, they are more than likely great people that have simply found themselves placed in the wrong job. I am not saying to go headhunting, what I am saying is this: You can either do this job or you cannot.

If you cannot, if you are not suited for this profession, then you should step aside for someone that is.

Companies can help greatly by letting go of and driving from their organizations these dated and flawed mindsets that: 1. The job of the safety practitioner is to manage safety also known as safety does safety! and, 2. The best way to accomplish that is via "Safety! Fix It!" As we have discussed, nothing good comes from these beliefs. We simply have a department or a person that is going around fixing and covering up learning opportunities. We are growing a work force that is dependent upon a sole practitioner or small group of practitioners to manage risk and/or take care of problems for them. There are a lot of holes in that approach, but try this one on for size: Rather than growing a risk knowledgeable and adaptive work force we are encouraging the transfer of risk from one person to another; from an employee that does the work to a safety person that does not do the work. We are moving the decision-making authority from an individual that knows how to do the work to someone that has a book that tells them how to do the work. Yes, it is as dumb and dangerous as it sounds. By doing so, we are removing expertise and "know-how." We are diluting ownership and diminishing personal responsibility. We are not accomplishing anything beneficial for our companies or our people. This creation of dependence also creates more and more safety bureaucracy, slowing down work and killing efficiency. All the while we are not actually doing anything substantial to better protect workers; we are more than likely causing harm. As a company, one of the best things that you can do to make things immediately better for everyone is to cut this cancer from your organization.

Companies that employ safety practitioners can also help with this by closely examining how they are finding, hiring, and retaining safety practitioners. We will take a deeper dive into the "care and feeding" of safety professionals in later chapters. But companies should be including their seasoned safety practitioners and safety managers in the process. Often, this process is commandeered by, or blindly turned over to an organization's human resources department. They tend to not quite grasp how to find good safety professionals. They look in the same places that you would seek HR specialist or engineers. To make matters worse, they often approach the search with the "anyone can do safety" mindset. So, this is what a job post typically ends up looking like:

ESSENTIAL DUTIES, RESPONSIBILITIES AND QUALIFICATIONS:

- Minimum 2 years of experience managing regulations
- Be committed to safety and team excellence.
- Be personable, professional, responsive, and bring value to the business.
- Have at least an Associate's degree and 3 years of related work experience.
- Be successful at building and maintaining strong relationships.
- Exercise strong communication skills both verbal and written.
- Be willing to travel throughout their assigned areas.
- Be able to work individually and in team environments.
- Ability to learn and adapt to new technologies and equipment.
- Frequent regional travel.

- Occasional overnight travel.
- Ensuring all employees follow local, state and federal regulations.
- Routinely inspecting and/or facilities to detect existing hazards.
- Performing periodic safety, environmental, and other regulatory audits.
- Assess and recommend controls to environmental aspects and impacts.
- Organize, file, and maintain large amounts of records.
- Able to evaluate unsafe situations, conditions and behaviors of others
- Document and track observations and other tasks and activities to completion.
- Travels from site to site within assigned area.
- Reports findings and suggests corrections for any safety violations found.
- Manages corrective actions.
- Investigates incidents for root cause(s) and propose actions.
- Demonstrates proper use of safety equipment.
- Review and confirm/update of all licenses and permit information.
- Review training files for all employees.
- Maintain the reporting/tracking software/database
- Assist and review training and mentoring.
- Any other duties and responsibilities may be assigned.

Are you awake? I would bet a significant amount of money that the last safety job your organization posted had a job description that sounded eerily similar, huh? We cast this net and we are surprised when we get bottles, cans, and other trash, rather than big, juicy fish. Here, I can translate this pretty quickly for you:

ESSENTIAL DUTIES, RESPONSIBILITIES AND QUALIFICATIONS:

- A little experience needed.
- Safety is the safety persons responsibility.
- We are hiring you to take care of employee safety, so we do not have to.
- Oh, and on top of that, we need you to do a bunch of other stuff

There, I fixed it! When I read these job descriptions, that is what I see. That is what a lot of good safety practitioners see as well. Many amazing, handsomely qualified, and experienced safety practitioners would not apply to the job posted above. It oozes "Safety! Fix It!" and most of us have learned how to spot and avoid "Safety! Fix It!" organizations. We must teach the organizations that employee safety professionals how to find them; how to find people with the right underlying beliefs about safety and the right skills. We must teach them how to attract them and how to retain them.

To rid ourselves of "Safety! Fix It!" we must start with the right organizational mindsets and the right mindsets as practitioners. As safety practitioners we must first stop creating and growing the ideology ourselves. We must let go of this need for control and this need for increased safety bureaucracy. Our existence must be justified by our professional ability and what we bring to the table, not by demanding we sign paperwork or that we be given first shot at changing toilet paper rolls in the bathrooms. We cannot create a dependent "Safety! Fix It!" cult and then be surprised when people actually join. We must pass on this knowledge and guidance to new and upcoming safety practitioners. We have done them a disservice and allowed them to mistakenly promote many of these flawed beliefs; the same mistaken and flawed beliefs that we ourselves promoted when we were new to the field. We have a responsibility to show them the way, the way that we had to learn on our own. We must work with our organizations to hire and retain the right safety practitioners, and we must challenge the existing "Safety! Fix It!" mindsets in our organizations. Organizations must turn away from these ideologies; they must excise them from their culture. Companies need to seek to understand the role of a safety person and should support their safety professionals. Companies and safety practitioners alike must awaken to the fact that these beliefs, while they seem very seductive and easy, only cause harm to their organizations and their employees. Safety practitioners included.

Know-it-all

We have just started down the weird, wild and wonky life of being a safety professional; we have just scratched the surface so far. Trust me, it will get weirder and wackier. Here is another fun fact: You are usually expected to be a subject matter expert on everything. And when I say everything, yes, I mean everything. That is right, from port-a-jon placement to asbestos removal; you are it! The people you work with will look at you like you are stupid when you do not know the regulatory requirements around an Inline 175A-CV3 Modulator Valve off the top of your head. You will hear "God, what kind of safety person are you! You don't even know what an Inline 175A-CV3 Modulator Valve is!" "Who let you be a safety person? You can't even tell me about the regulations surrounding the placement and continued servicing of portable toilets!" You have heard something similar; I am sure of it. In those situations, you can feel your hands inching closer to their necks as they spew this ill-informed garbage in your direction, I completely get it. While strangling these people would seem like the next logical step in these types of interactions, it is not. We first must cut them some slack. It is not entirely their fault; some blame belongs to the organizations in which you find this mindset. A harder pill to swallow is the fact that some of this is our fault as well. It should be obvious that some of this comes from the "Safety! Fix It!" mindsets we just discussed. They can be closely related and sometimes linked; they probably originate in the same places. But here we will explore some slightly different paths and how to (hopefully) begin to overcome these know-it-all views placed upon the safety profession.

As mentioned, I do not simply fling blame upon those that perpetuate these myths. Leaders, managers, and executives that demonstrate these beliefs are often caught up in an organizations underlying beliefs about the role of safety practitioners. They are simply caught up in the "myth of the safety professional;" this myth that says to be a good safety practitioner one must be the "all-knowing great wise one." But they do hold some levels of responsibility and we need to talk about it. They have a few mentionable areas for improvement; they continue to lean on the safety practitioner as a "great knower," as a shaman, a profit, or a guru. Not only do they rely on them as a sole source of information, they also lean on a safety person or safety department to fix their problems for them (Safety! Fix It!). A good deal of this comes from laziness; but some derives from a place of more malicious intent. Let's be totally honest, a good portion of people do not crave self-reliance. In fact, they often desire the total opposite; these people desire dependence. They hold this thought that "the more you do for me, the less I must do overall. I also lose a significant amount of personal risk. If things go wrong, I can blame you. It will be your fault and not mine." And boom, just like that, we are back to "safety does safety, so I do not have to do safety" because who the hell has time for that anyways, right? To continue, a bit of this problem is simply egotistical masculine bull shit. "See everyone, I know more than the safety person. I am strong and smart! Look at my dominance! Look at my superiority! Me Smart!" Either way, it is stupid. One of the quickest ways to begin to challenge this myth is to start lightly pushing back. You do not have to challenge it by jumping on your desk, ripping off your shirt, and screaming "that is not my job!" Although, I am a fan of that method. Just challenge people to do things on their own; force self-reliance. When someone brings you a "know-it-all" question or submits an inquiry to the guru, send them on a quest to find the answers for themselves. Send them off into the wilderness and ask them to bring you back the solution. This method is one of my favorite ways to draw them into the hunt for information and force self-reliance. This is pretty similar to the old "teach them how to fish" method which works well too.

I do not lay blame at the feet of those leaders and managers really. The setting that the organization and industry has created drives their behavior; their views on the role of a safety practitioner is not something that they have just made up on their own. The underlying beliefs of the organization and of industry in general have driven them to the conclusions that they have formed. Yes, once they are made aware of the B.S. they should cut the B.S. But it is not quite that simple; if we want real change we must focus on the underlying beliefs and assumptions that our organizations and industries hold about safety as a profession. We must adequately redefine the role of the safety practitioner, removing our profession from the guru or "know-it-all" categories.

Do not think for a moment that we safety professionals will escape this one unscathed. There are a lot of people within our profession that think of themselves in the terms that we have just described. Many out there want to be known as the know-it-all, some want to the guru, and they want the workforces that they support to be dependent upon them. It makes sense why; the feeling of being needed, the feeling of job security, and the feeling of importance. It makes complete and total sense that we end up with some safety professionals that are OSHA compliance shaman; that people must go up on high to the sacred safety office to find answers – that they must get their answers from the great "safety knower!" The dependence that they have created to make themselves feel relevant has only been harmful. Consolidating and centralizing safety information is simply ineffective and dangerous. For those in our profession that continue to promote this way of thinking; we have no room for gurus in this line of work. Go be the know-it-all elsewhere; we do not need you.

The problem is that you will never know everything; you should not seek to know everything. You should not be required to know everything! You should not be required to memorize (or keep a copy of) the regulations of safe portable toilet management. Those guru safety folks we were just picking on, no matter how well they pretend to know everything, they do not. They know some and the rest they recklessly "shoot from the hip." A lot of my beef comes from the fact that, rather than spreading knowledge and information, we attempt to centralize knowledge and information. We try to simplify and centralize knowledge and information; giving its power to a select few "chosen" people. We create barriers to this desperately needed information, by doing so we create the guru class within our workforces. To make matters worse, this select few have rarely, if ever, done the actual work. So, in essence, we are taking the power of knowledge and information away from those that do work and placing it in the hands of those that do not We are taking away the expectation that "those that do" seek out and obtain knowledge about what it is that they do. Rather, we have gurus and "great knowers" hoard needed and vital information and dispense it back to "those that do" upon request. How ridiculous is that?

Safety professionals should not, they must not, be relied upon as "know-it-alls" or gurus. It is as stupid as it is harmful. We must drive deference to expertise; we must be willing to rely on subject matter experts and defer to "those that do" to make decisions. We must force employee self-reliance; we must "teach people how to fish." Me must show employees how to find the information that they seek rather than squirreling information away so that we might sound a little smarter and more important later.

It's so easy anyone can do it

In an imaginary land far, far away XYZ Corporation is hiring. They are looking for an environmental position, they end up hiring a heavily qualified environmental professional with 9 years of experience. This environmental scientist is sharp; tons of education and seems pretty fun to boot. Soon they find themselves looking for an engineer, they hire a heavily qualified engineer, this person has over 20 years of experience. She has won industry awards and been featured in various trade journals. They broke the pay-scale to secure her; rightfully so. XYZ Corporation has really been expanding, they are now hiring a human resources manager. They end up hiring an amazing HR professional with 15 years of experience. He knows his stuff and really cares about people. He does not even seem to mind when they call him the human remains manager. With all this growth XYZ Corporation started to have some safety problems. Last week they were audited by OSHA and received a few citations. A month before that they had a pretty significant injury; an employee is still in the hospital. They did what any innovative and forward-thinking large corporation would do, they asked their industry peers what they should do. They were swiftly advised to hire a safety person. So XYZ Corporation hired a safety person. What were their qualifications you might ask? Oh, none. Years of experiences? Well they have been working for a couple of years; not in safety or anything. Think faster and think food. God, stop asking questions! Heck, anyone can do safety! It's the director's cousin, we hired the director's cousin - they start tomorrow.

Cold-hard fact: "Anyone Can Do Safety" Mindsets are Prevalent. Environmental position = Heavily qualified environmental professional, Engineering position = Heavily qualified engineer, Human Resources Position = Heavily qualified human remains professional, Safety position = someone's freaking cousin. A funny story about that...

I was doing a quick turnaround job down South; it was about a 4 week gig. It was a pretty good job honestly. The pay was good, there was as much overtime as you could ever want, and it was short! I'd be back in Virginia on a lake fishing pretty quick; hopefully with a pocket full of cash. After driving most of the day to get to the site, I finally arrived. I processed through security and made my way to the site training center. I checked-in at the front desk "Good afternoon sir, I'm reporting to John Doe the safety director. I'm the contract safety guy" I said. "Great! Mr. Doe will be glad you made it!" he said. He then guided me to a computer. I quickly knocked out the required training and mandatory safety orientation and made my way towards the safety office. I slowly opened the door, sticking my head in and saying "Mr. Doe?" All three people in the safety office looked up at me at the same time. A gentleman in the back said "which one?"

Hopefully by now you are piecing together where this is going. They were all related; there were three Mr. Does in that office. It was the "Doe department" – There was Grandpa Doe, Father Doe, and Son Doe, they were the safety department. It was almost comical; they didn't even try to hide it. I heard "Hey dad, come take a look at this for me" more times than I can count. I'm not picking on them, they were actually really great people. But I am calling out the practice, it's bull shit!

Here is a really crazy idea, let's hire safety professionals to be safety professionals. Look, I get it, everyone needs a place to start. But, taking a kid fresh off the fryer and making them a safety manager, that's about as dumb as it gets. There, I said it. It's dumb, its stupid, and it's dangerous. I do not care whose cousin they are. Everyone deserves a start, but they need to start in the right position. A great place to start that fry cook, that frontline employee, that tradesperson that wants to give safety a shot, is as a safety tech. It's an amazing place to learn and grow. I started as a tech in a department with four safety professionals and a manager. These folks were epic. They came from amazingly diverse backgrounds and had about 90 years of experience between them. they each had a long and winding road that led them to the profession. That little group had everything from a college graduate to a high school dropout and I learned something from each of them. They took me under their wings, they taught me the right way to do things, and I listened. That small group of people taught me many lessons that I still use to this day. It was an amazing experience that I cherish, one that every entry level safety professional should experience. On that note, I'm the last person that will tell you that safety professionals need a couple of masters degrees, an internship, 14 letters of recommendation, 47 letters after their name, and 120 years of experience in the field; I think a lot of the requirements we put on safety pros are bull shit in general.

I had been working in the field for a while; I was still green. I was just more of a dark hunter green than a bright neon green by this point in my career. I was working for a large contractor company; this was one of those massive organizations where you never really meet the leadership team. I honestly did not think they actually existed. I assumed that they were some form of animatronics that the company used to make us believe that we actually had a leadership team. So, you can imagine my shock and disbelief when I received an email stating that the vice president of environmental health and safety was coming to visit our remote little site. The visit was scheduled a week from the day that I received the email; that is not a lot of time to prepare in the power plant world. One week later, D day, I am standing out in the site parking lot with the rest of the management team waiting for the vice president to arrive. I remember how funny it was to watch a parade of black SUV's roll up to this small fossil power plant in the middle of nowhere. It looked like a presidential motorcade; the only thing missing were those little flags on the fenders. I do not know your life experiences; a gaggle of black SUV's usually does not mean anything good where I come from. It looked like something out of a movie. They rolled up through the front gate, blowing past security and parking directly in front of our job site trailer. We all quickly scurried over to greet the vice president and his team. Assistants and the accompanying staff all poured from the SUV's and started opening doors and grabbing bags. It seemed like a hundred people came out; eventually we could see the VP. As his assistants were trying to help him from the SUV, you could hear him shouting "get your damn hands off of me, I'm old, I ain't dead!" And just like that, there he was. He was a portly Texan standing about 4'9", he was wearing a 10-gallon hat, a massive belt buckle, and alligator boots. As he straightened out his clothes, brushing out the wrinkles from his shirt, he turned to his assistants and said with a deep drawl, "I'm sorry for getting grumpy, you know how I get when I travel." And off we went! There was no time to waste, we had much corporate bull shit to attend to. We had meeting after meeting and audit after audit, the day just seemed to drag by. Through the entire day I hoped to get a few moments with the VP. I wanted to pick his brain, I wanted to ask him some questions – safety person to safety person.

It was our final meeting and we had just wrapped up. He was standing there by himself. I finally had my time alone with the vice president. I was running through all the questions I should ask in my head. This was a big deal; I did not want to squander the opportunity to learn from this guy. Putting the theatrics from earlier aside, he seemed like a pretty down to earth guy. He had impressed me with his quickness to apologize to his staff. His success was inspiring; he had clearly gone about as far as you could go as a safety practitioner, at least within a single company. So, I wanted the opportunity to learn from him. Here is that interaction: I asked, "what type of training or education should a safety professional seek to continue to grow in our profession?" I continued, "I really aspire to grow professionally and to continue to climb the ladder, what tips could you give me?" He paused for a moment, seemingly to gather his thoughts and then he said with a deep southern drawl "None of them!" he continued "You can either do this job or you can't – It's really as simple as that." I was a little stunned, that wasn't what I was expecting to hear. He then said, "If you work hard and do right by people, the sky is the limit." He walked off and wandered into another conversation and I never saw him again. Those words have always stuck with me.

Here is the learning I extracted from that interaction; I have tried my best to apply it to my life: a) Don't judge a book by its cover or by its education level. There are so many great people out there that would make amazing safety professionals. Sure, they need a little TLC, they need a little training, they need a good mentor, and no, they shouldn't start as a lone safety professional or safety manager. Don't limit your hiring options based on outdated and ineffective educational constructs and experience requirements. Requirements that some person with a useless and expensive degree created long, long ago to justify their own, expensive and useless degree. My "long and winding road" to this profession made me the professional I am today. On paper, I would have never guessed it would have ended up in safety and human performance. When I was hired as a tech, I was a nuclear outage coater that worked as a firefighter/EMT on the side and was formally educated in criminal justice. Doesn't that just scream future safety professional? Before you get too mad, I'm not putting down traditional means of education. But I am not so sure that if I had gone into a traditional EH&S college program and interned, that I would have gained the same level of knowledge and "know-how." This brings us full circle: You can either do this job or you cant. Give people a shot, a shot in the right position, and mentor and guide them. Plant them, water them, and see if they bloom into a pretty safety flower. b) Be good to people, treat people like people, and keep your word to them. To grossly oversimplify this, work hard and don't be a shithead. But really, just be good to people and treat them with kindness. It's all about that "golden rule" our mothers and fathers taught us (or beat into us). Treat others how you want to be treated. c) Combining those words of

54

wisdom; If you discover that you have a knack for this wonky job, you are good to people, and you work hard, anything is possible. The sky really is the limit.

We need to cut the shit! We need to hire the right people to fill safety jobs. That does not mean that we cannot give "green" or inexperienced people an opportunity. In fact, I think we need more of that. We need more people entering this profession at a tech level, being mentored by quality safety professional, and then churned out into the "real world." We need to think about the future; we are not getting any younger. We need to make things better for the next generation of safety people. We need to have a hand in shaping the next generation, we need to pass on the lessons we have learned. We must stamp out this "anyone can do safety" mentality. We must take a stand against it anytime that it rears its ugly head. We should lash out against it and demand that the same level of care that is given to hiring an engineer or an HR specialist is applied in the search to fill safety roles. We must challenge the old methods that we use to find safety people, we must rethink outdated and ineffective educational constructs and experience requirements. I'm all for education and training, but there are many ways to gain knowledge. In our modern world, many of the best ways to gain knowledge do not reward you with a fancy piece of paper to hang on the wall. When it comes right down to it, you can either do this job or you cannot. If you can, you work hard and you are good to people, you will go pretty far

I report to who!?!

     An unfortunate truth about this profession, one that you need to understand, is that your reporting structure will always be murky. There are only a few safety gigs out there that have a "clean" reporting scheme; most are pretty wonky. It is rare, unicorn rare, if you find yourself in a true "safety department." Finding a department with real teammates, a real manager, all based at the same location, is practically unheard of in this profession. Most of us find ourselves assigned to sites or locations that are far removed from other safety professionals or safety leaders. We are usually it. We are often a lone wolf; a safety department of one. Sure, you will have a direct "safety manger," they are kind-of-sort-of your manager. They usually handle normal managerial things like signing time sheets and keeping up with your required training. But that's typically where things end. Often, they are based out of some corporate office far, far away. You will rarely, if ever have daily or weekly contact with them. This manager will typically only get involved with you when they are required to. Your phone will ring only to hear about go-dos, complaints, or problems. Your "manager" is usually more of a mediator than a manager; patching up problems between you and the leadership of the location in which you find yourself. On top of that you will likely have "dotted line" reporting to a few other leaders. You will report to a location or site manager, an operations manager, and sometimes more. In the worst of the worst organizations, safety professionals will report into human resources. How stupid is that? What is the best part of all this wackiness? They will constantly fight over who you "really" work for; they will all think that they are your boss. They will yell and scream about who gets to decide what you do, where you go, what hours you work, and everything else. Sounds like an absolute blast, right? But wait, there is more! In addition to your "solid line" reporting and your "dotted line" reporting, everyone else will think that they are your boss, too. Oh, and if you do not agree with them and take their orders, that means "you don't care!" And a safety professional that is labeled as "not caring" will soon find themselves looking for their next assignment.

A funny tale about fighting over who controls you as a safety professional. I was working as a regional safety manager for a large maintenance and construction contractor in the southwest. It was a pretty good company; mostly great people just trying to "GSD" ("get shit done" for those of you that have not been in the field). The leadership team was a completely different story. You see, this organization had experienced some leadership struggles over the past year. They had exchanged the top two leaders, the regional director and manager to be exact, with new and much worse leaders. Sounds like the normative corporate response to something, eh? I remember my first introduction to the new regional director well. I walked in and greeted the gentleman, "how are you today sir? Welcome to our group. It is a pleasure to meet you." He responded quickly and in a very demeaning tone "So you are the safety guy, huh? I've never met one of those that I have liked, and you won't be the first." Talk about a first impression! The new regional manager was pretty lackluster as well; primarily acting as the henchman for the regional director. They were quite the pair; they drove that office into the ground. Seriously, the branch closed within a year of their takeover. They forced great employees to flee and ruined relationships with prized clients. The saying rings true, "People Don't Leave Bad Jobs, They Leave Bad Bosses." But that is not the story for today.

My story begins here; the branch in which I was located was going to be presented several awards at an upcoming get together. This event was a big deal within the company; it was massive. Massive both in size and importance. This was the organization's annual "Summit of Excellence!" Pretty impressive, right? They had mixers, famous speakers and personalities, they offered exclusive training sessions and seminars, and to top off this weeklong extravaganza, they held a huge black-tie awards ceremony.

Those that were selected to go, got plenty of "face time" with higher ups in the company; getting to rub elbows with executives and senior leaders. On a related side note: everything, and I mean everything, has some political element to it. As bull shit as it is in most cases, politics matter. They especially matter when you are fighting for positive change in a broken system while reporting to five different people. Politics influence these wonky reporting structures that we are talking about. You need to understand the politics, understand the political landscape in which you find yourself, work through them, work around them, and never let politics prevent you from doing the right things. But, back to the story at hand. My work in the branch had been noticed from "up on high;" the senior director of EH&S had personally requested that I attend the summit and accept certain safety related awards on behalf of the facilities that I represented (safety awards are bull shit too, but that is another book entirely). I was excited by the opportunity to finally meet some of my peers in the company and to hobnob with the big dogs; who wouldn't be? I was in a remote location far, far, and I mean far away. I was still pretty unknown outside of our little branch, so I felt very lucky to be invited and fortunate to have the opportunity.

I quickly began clearing my calendar, making my travel arrangements, planning things to do while there, and setting up my "out of office" note. That is where things start to go awry; I sent the team an email detailing my time out office. It was your normal "hey I'll be gone a week email." It went a little something like this: "Team – I will be out office attending the Summit of Excellence. You can reach me via email or phone. I will be checking both periodically so do not hesitate to reach out. Have a great week!" Not too shabby, huh? Within 5 minutes of pressing send, I could hear heavy and fast footsteps coming down the hall. You could almost feel the low muffled steps through the carpeted floors. It did not hit me yet what was coming for me. The regional director stormed into my office; he started yelling before he made it through the door. "What in gods good name do you think you are doing?" I was shocked but attempted to formulate a reply, "what do you mean, sir?" "The Summit of Excellence? You are not going to that shit!" he continued "if I can do without a safety person around here for a week, I do not need one at all!" I was getting angry at this point; I had found my breaking point with these guys. I did not tell you that in the months leading up to this interaction, these gentleman had cut our safety funding to the bone. This had resulted in the layoffs of multiple safety positions and left the few remaining in the department (myself included) running ragged. I said, "listen and listen well, the senior director of EH&S invited me and I am going. If you have a problem with that take it up with him." He quickly snapped back "oh I will, and I'll have your paycheck for this! You will either be fired, or I'll quit!" as he stormed out the regional manager entered; his henchman had arrived. I was standing between my desk and the door as he rushed me while saying in a stern voice "what is this? Who the hell do you think you are? You are not going to this thing! We have already decided that." I decided that it was time to respond to "ass hole" by being a bigger ass hole. I looked the man square in the eyes and said "Fuck off! It's not your call." He looked shocked and bewildered; I continued "I do not know who the hell you think you are. We are both managers, you are not the boss in this situation. Hell, even with the regional director, it's not his call. So, neither of you have the right or backing to decide where I can or cannot go. So, we are back to my first response, fuck off." He drew closer, he was angry and turning red. He poked me in the chest saying, "that's it, you are done here buddy!" my response is probably what you would expect; it was what most would do if an angry man were poking you in the chest. I calmly said, "if you ever do that again, I'll break your god damn finger off." Probably not the wisest choice of words but well warranted either way, and lucky for him I did not actually break it off. This is the kind of bull shit that happens when we insist that safety professional (or anyone for that matter) report to 5 different people. Murky reporting appeases those leaders that desire control, but it does not do us any favors. It is detrimental to working relationships and simply results in confusion and arguments.

The story ends on a much brighter note; I will give away some of the ending now for those that are wondering. I went to the Summit of Excellence, I met some amazing people, and I had a great time. As for the remainder of our colorful cast of players, they were not quite as lucky. After our alteration, the regional manager promptly reported my "threat of physical harm" to human resources (certain that it would get me fired) who instantly launched an inquiry (rightfully so) into the issue. After detailing what had occurred to human resources, they were baffled, "wait, he put his hands on you?" I replied "well, yeah he was in my face poking me in the chest." The HR specialist then responded "Wow, you really should have ripped his god damn finger off. We're done here." He was transferred and demoted before the end of the day. The last I had heard; he was acting as a personal assistant to a low-level manager at a location somewhere back east. The regional director did a little better, although he did not keep his promise and quit. He was forced into an early retirement a few months later and no one has really heard from him since. I stuck around for a while; sinking ships are not a good place to hang around for long. I left for a competitor just before the office closed.

There are a couple of key points that I want to pull out of this story: a) This "safety reports to everyone" style of reporting is ineffective and harmful. It leads to confusion for those down the line and leads to pissing contests between leaders. It is bull shit and it must go. b) Having good leaders above you can mean everything to your success or failure. In this situation and many others, having amazing and strong leaders in my chain of command made all the difference in the world. Having an amazing director, one that was willing to have my back, was my only saving grace. Good leaders are a great thing! But we should not have to rely on them as the only line of defense to keep this from happening. So where do we go from here?

Let's start by addressing the reporting structure of safety professionals; how they report and who they should report to. First and foremost, we must admit that the current structure must go. I get that it is not going anywhere overnight, but It is not even an option that we keep it in the long run. I think a really good starting point is to address (and somewhat readdress) what the role of a safety professional should be. Understanding that role has significant implications on the reporting scheme. To grossly oversimply the role of a safety practitioner, they should be consultants. We need to assess, think, provided possible solutions, give guidance, bring a different perspective, and be facilitators of learning. Again, there is more. There is a lot more that we could get into attempting to define the perfect description of a safety professional. Maybe it is better to understand why we find ourselves in these weird reporting arrangements to begin with. We find ourselves in the "safety reports to everyone" structure for several different reasons, some of which we have already touched on. Some of it is a control thing. Managers and leaders always want you and everyone else under their thumbs. The thought of an employee, especially some "safety puke," on their site or in their shop that does not report to them, drives them up the wall. Much has to do with our organizational mindsets around safety as a profession. If "Safety! Fix It!" is your plan for addressing issues, then everyone telling your safety professional what to do, where to go, and how to do it, probably makes sense. If safety is your subject matter expert for everything and everyone, yep, it probably makes sense. If your organization holds the "anyone can do safety" mindset; believing that safety is a mindless task and that safety professionals are to not be trusted. Yes, it would make senses that your professionals would require as much oversite and direction as you can give them. We end up here for a few different reasons, but all of those reasons are bull shit. So first, I believe we need to address those issues if we want long lasting betterment. But we must ultimately change how safety professionals report in our organizations.

I have seen and experienced a couple of different structures that work well. I know that we could debate this topic for hours and hours. I also realize that there is not a "magic bullet" that would work well for every organization; organizations are far too unique for that to be the case. But I want to outline some good practices that I have seen in my time. One structure that seems to work well, is to have the safety function report as its own business unit. Let us line this out from bottom to top. A safety tech would report to a site safety manager who would then report to a regional safety manager. That regional safety manager would report to a safety director who would then report to a vice president of safety, EH&S, EHS&S or similar. That VP would then report up to the president, CEO, or similar role. Some of the major benefits here: a) The safety structure mirrors the businesses operations structure. You have equal amounts of power on both sides of the fence. This helps to settle conflicts rather quickly; people feel equal as they are dealing with each other. b) We lose the obvious issue of a murky reporting structure. This is about as clean as it gets, reporting directly up without all of the B.S. "dotted line" reporting. Command and control is easy to understand; demands and orders come down through the structure rather than from all over. One major con to these styles of reporting is that it can make your safety department even more of an "outsider." This is since the team is completely separate from the operations teams. But, with good solid leaders and quality safety professionals, I have seen this hurdle quickly eliminated.

Another commonly successful reporting structure is the operations support style of reporting. Let me explain what I mean; safety basically rolls up under a high-level operations support director. This director often reports directly to a vice president of a business unit, a VP of operations support, or similar. Operations support is often comprised of training, safety, health services, human performance, and other support functions. This structure can be applied as one operations support group for the entire company or as individual operations support groups for each business unit in the organization. Either way, I have seen it work well for a few different reasons: a) safety is viewed as support; as consultants rather than owners of safety. This helps to place safety ownership where it truly belongs, with operations. b) as with the previous example, it helps to eliminate confusion. c) it is easier for some organizations to stomach this hierarchy because it is more cost efficient. You have a single director for multiple support functions. A con to this style is that the VP in which the operations support unit plugs into has a dramatic effect on the group. If the VP's beliefs about safety (or any other function within the group) are not-so-great, the function can be rendered useless or thrust back to where it started.

Those are just a couple of options to think about. But no matter what reporting hierarchy your organization chooses for safety, here are some things to avoid: a) dotted line reporting in general. It is stupid and causes confusion. One effective leader is better than five that have been rendered useless by each other. b) Anything that diminishes the sense of team or community. c) Allowing flawed mindsets and beliefs about safety as a profession to persist in the organization and influence the reporting structure of safety professionals. d) Having safety report into human resource. This immediately compromises trust of the safety professional, as they are seen as being part of the disciplinary structure. Safety and human resources should be like oil and water – they should not mix. And, e) anything that dilutes structural clarity; leading to confusion and frustration for everyone involved.

Murky and confusing reporting structures cause harm within organizations. We would never dilute the chain of command for other professions or functions. Do companies require that an operations manager report to three different directors and two other managers? Nope. Do companies require that a maintenance manager report to a site manager, a corporate maintenance manager, to an HR manager, and a director? That is a big fat no. So why then, when we add the magical word "safety" in there, does all that change? The safety profession deserves the same clean and clear reporting structure that other functions receive. We need the same clarity in our chain of command. There are a multitude of different ways to solve this problem; way more than we have covered here. But I will challenge you with this. If your organization employs safety professionals or support staff of any kind really, take a look at the structure. Is it working? Is it really working? We need to take some time to step back and look. We need to take a fresh and meaningful look at how safety as a profession fits within our organizations. It is the right thing to do, for both the safety practitioners and the companies in which they work. The potential betterment that could be brought about for our profession, could help other professions as well. Those that find themselves in similar reporting situations such as environmental professionals and human performance professionals. The structure and leadership of safety practitioners plays a big part into how successful they are and into an organizations ability to retain quality practitioners and cultivate effective safety leaders.

Work > Life

Look, work sucks. Work sucks for everyone. How does that saying go? "That's why they call it work." But I think we all are waking up to the fact that work should suck a whole lot less. For some reason, that thinking has not progressed to the safety profession. Our group is one of the last holdouts in the "work should suck" camp. Our companies think our lives should suck; we think our lives should suck. We still seem to believe that things should be awful, and they must be as awful as possible! We persist in the belief that we should harm our mental health, our personal relationships, and overall personal well-being to earn a paycheck. For some safety folks, I believe they think it makes the profession more "noble." Our employers must just be sadist pricks. There is a lot of B.S. that contributes to our "work sucks" problem. Much of what we have talked about in the previous chapters contributes significantly to this problem. So yes, some of this issue is more symptomatic than it is causal. Some of it is the result of shitty companies and some of it is self-inflicted. But, one thing is for certain, it is all bull shit and it must get better.

Let's start by talking about the elephant in the room, the balance problem. One of the biggest beefs I come across, and one of the biggest culprits, are the horrible hours that most safety pros face. Employers understaff safety departments all while insisting uninterrupted or near uninterrupted "safety coverage." Most of us have first-hand experience in how that ends up. We work night, day, and everything in between. We are always on-call; being expected to answer the phone or come back to work at any given moment. I have even heard of some safety professionals being fired for failing to answer a phone or respond to an email in the middle of the night. One of my favorite personal experiences (god, I hope my sarcasm is coming through in this thing) was with a company that demanded we (we being the safety department only) arrive to work one hour early and remain after for an additional hour. They labeled this as "professional time" and it was mandatory. It was not only mandatory, but it was also unpaid. That means if you are working a 10-hour shift, you would be required to work 12 hours while only being paid for 10. It was actually a pretty common practice for a while; you have probably noticed there are quite a few lawsuits nowadays from these shady cost-cutting practices. "Did you work for Imaginary XYZ Corporation between 2007 and 2016? Did you work hours that you were not compensated for? Call 1-800-WE-SUE-4-U now!" I really hope someone out there gives them hell; terrible and unethical companies deserve whatever bad befalls them. "Play stupid games, win stupid prizes." So, not only are you required to work ridiculously long hours, you will only be compensated for about half of them (if you are lucky). You will often be a one-person army, you will be the entire safety department, you will be a lone wolf . We all have our experiences with this bull shit, here is one of mine:

I had been working for a few months at a little power plant back east; it was a nice little coal plant. I had arrived in early January, so things had been pretty calm so far. For those out there that are unfamiliar with power generation, there are two primary busy seasons known as "outage seasons." One occurring in the spring and the other in the fall. This is when the plant will come offline to do maintenance, projects, and the like. I had arrived prior to the spring outage season so there was not a lot going on. But that was about to dramatically change. We had just started planning for the upcoming outage; we accomplished that like any good utility by conducting about a thousand "pre-outage" meetings. Folks were going on and on about staffing of additional supervisors, coverage for this and that, needing extra leaders so people can rotate days off, and other outage-related concerns. Things drew silent for a second; this was my moment. I took the opportunity to add my input for safety staffing. "From what I hear, it sounds like we will be ramping up to around 500 contractor and a few hundred internal personnel at the peak of this outage…" "Conservatively, I think we should bring in 3 or 4 contract safety professionals." I continued, "This number will give us adequate coverage and allow people to have a day off." "I'll get started loo.." The site manager interrupted, "Let me stop you right there, we're not bringing in any additional safety people. We didn't budget for it, sorry." I snapped back "We've committed to provide safety coverage; how do you expect that we do that?" he responded, "I don't expect us to do that, I expect you to do that." I spent the next 60 days working practically non-stop. I would wake up at 2:45 AM, shower and get ready, I'd be in my car by 3:15 AM, and at work by 3:30 AM. I would work until around noon, then I'd drive home and take a nap until 2:00 PM. I would be back to work by 2:30 PM and I'd work until at least 10:00 PM. I'd head home, grab a bite to eat, hit the sack, and repeat. And that was a good day! You heard that right, I was working anywhere between 16 to 18 hours every single day for over 60 days straight. I was so pissed off, physically spent, and emotionally burned out after that outage, but I stuck around. More about that in a few minutes.

When it comes to hours, safety professionals tend to get the shittiest end of the stick. It is not uncommon for safety professionals to work 80 to 90 hours every single week; with some organizations continuing to refuse to pay them overtime. I can't believe that we still live in a world in which we hide behind "you are salary!" or the "professional time" garbage, but we do. Projects are understaffed and underfunded. As I was made painfully aware, safety staffing is usually an afterthought. So, "duh," this often results in a single safety professional trying to cover a massive project that should have a small safety army. To compound these problems, a safety professional is usually leaned upon to cover the gaps created by lazy leaders and a gamut of additional organizational problems such as understaffing in other functional areas. It is not unheard of to stumble upon safety practitioners doing project scheduling, running crews, or tracking budgets, in addition to their primary functions. You will find that companies lay all kinds of wonky expectations upon their safety folks. Hell, at one point in my career, I came across a site safety manager that was expected to erect scaffolding for a portion of each of his shifts. Yes, you heard that correctly – he was a straight up "scaffologist" for 3 to 4 hours out of each day. I want this to come through loud and clear; HE WAS THE SITE SAFETY MANAGER. He was the leader of the site's safety organization, he had 5 direct reports, and he was expected to erect scaffolding. Simply put, a lot of companies do this because they do not value safety practitioners. They do not find value in safety as a profession, so they force the practitioner to do things that they believe are valuable. In this case, it was hanging scaffolding. If your company does this crap, your company sucks. No really, if you treat your professionals like this, you SUCK. While I never had too many extracurricular activities thrown my way, I did struggle for many years in the work/life balance department.

I had been in the safety profession for about 3 years when I had my first real bout with the balance monster.

The monster was always there, I was just too young and green to notice the problems yet. I was working as the safety manager for a massive nationally known contractor at that little fossil power plant I just mentioned. On top of working 16 to 18 hours every single day for over 60 days straight during that outage; the norm was to work at least 12 hours every day non-outage (only for safety people – the remainder of the leadership team were lucky to pull 30 actual hours a week). The normal site schedule was 4 - 10's but that never happened. The usual was 4 – 12's and sometimes 5 -12's and of course they only paid for 40 hours every week. What, do you think they were made of money!?! Look, I know I am griping about hours, but that is just the beginning of this story. This job was a combination platter of bull shit. On top of the frustration of working a lot of hours that I would never be paid for, this site took an extreme psychological toll. It was one of those places in which safety practitioners were not only undervalued, they were despised. They were hated, especially by the management team. This ideology of hatred for safety practitioners trickled down and was mirrored by every layer of the organization. I vividly recall a situation in which one of our subcontractor's safety professionals was spit on by one of our employees. The reason? He asked him to wear safety glasses. What was leaderships reaction, you ask? "The safety person should have asked nicer." Horrible, right? Well that pretty much sums up this site in a nutshell. It was a Mod Podge of awful leaders, even worse managers, and terrible practices.

74

You see, this site was a little odd. Well, not that odd in the contractor space, but probably odd for those that have not been involved with power generation contractors. As I mentioned, I worked for a contractor, we were THE contractor for the site. It is a pretty common practice in power generation to hire a maintenance and construction contractor; that contractor handles the brunt of the plants work. They had been using this method for years to get things done. Contract companies had come, and they had gone. Within the past 10 years they had changed companies four times. You see, these issues were not new and (obviously) they were not completely isolated to safety. The owners of the plant had taken notice; they had taken notice about four times. Their solution to the issue was to boot one contract company off-site and bring in another. The problem, they never actually changed leadership or people at the site level. People would literally just change hardhats, purge their offices of the previous company's swag, and start getting checks from a different corporation. It was sort of a running joke; you could accurately determine a person's tenure by the hardhats hanging in their offices. You could count the different company hardhats just like counting rings on a tree. So, mindsets never really changed; nothing ever really changed. The site had a safety position because their last couple of corporate overseers required them to have one. Plus, their client now required them to keep one. It had good optics for the client, and they liked having someone around to blame when things went wrong for the contractor.

After a year of this, I was on the verge of walking away. I was done, I was over it, and I was ready to move on. Not only from this site, but from the profession all together. What was the straw that broke the camels back? I had just left a meeting in which I had been blamed (publicly tarred and feathered for over an hour) for an event that occurred. I had just finished a phone call with the client in which they demanded that I provide them with MY corrective actions and MY complete report (including a root cause, mind you) within 12 hours. I remember the call well "You better tell me how you are going to fix this Goodman!" I had just spent the last 12-months of my life working my fingers to the bone trying to pull this horrific site out of the stone-age. My reward was to be the scapegoat for shitty managers over an event; to take the blame and mop up the problem for everyone. That was enough for me, I was officially burned out. I walked to my office, grabbed a few things, and walked out to my car. As I was standing there cussing god and preparing to drive off into the sunset, I called my manager. My manager worked out of the main corporate office; the corporate office was only about 1,000 miles away. I never spent much face to face time with the gentleman, but he was a great manager and a great person in general. I blew my top; I went full-on "vent mode" on him. He just listened and listened, and that was exactly what I needed in that moment. He finally spoke up "look, don't quit. You do not want to quit. If you quit you won't get to see things get better." I'm listening to this thinking "better? Yeah right!" He said "really, give me a chance to fix this. If I cannot fix it, I will personally help you find a job somewhere else – hell, I'll give you mine! Just give me a month." I agreed. This moment, for whatever reason, was what it took to wake up the company to the problems of this location. Within those 30 days the site had a new site manager and several new leaders. Not just new, but good. When I close my eyes and imagine the qualities of a good site director or manager, the person they hired comes to mind. It was exactly what the site needed, it changed everything. The site got better, it got dramatically better. I did not stick around for too much longer after this, I was eventually promoted and left the location. I was off to conquer the corporate world. It was hard, but I left things better than how I found them. But It took me a long time to mentally and emotionally recover from that plant. It is not easy to admit, but I was depressed, I was scarred, I was "damaged goods." I think that is where we need to start; the first step to overcoming a problem is admitting the problem exists.

First, we need to admit that this neglect of the practitioner's overall health and wellbeing is completely unacceptable. Secondly, we need to actually do something about it. I am completely done with seeing safety professionals die young of heart attacks, strokes, or suicide. I am tired of watching people lose their relationships because of this job, I am over watching people suffer at work because we refuse to do anything about it, and I'm sick of witnessing the depression that exists within our profession. We simply pretend that the problem does not exist, all the while we have professionals suffering. We stick our heads in sand and squawk "but that's the way it's always been done!" We have professionals turning to alcohol or drugs to deal with occupation induced depression. People are taking out their frustrations on their families and loved ones, ruining marriages and personal relationships. Some are so depressed that they cannot even get out of bed. So yeah, it is bull shit and we must do better. I will be the first to admit that I do not know all the fixes. But I do know that we have a serious problem. A problem that will require us to spend a good amount of time focusing on the "care and feeding" of the safety professional. An area that has been long neglected by our employers, our professional associations, and even ourselves. Individually, we need to do a better job of asking for help. We need to do a better job of leaning on each other and looking out for each other's wellbeing. Employers need to focus on providing safety professionals with work/life balance. We should not be excluded, as we often are, from these much needed and sometimes lifesaving necessities. Our professional associations should focus on challenging the "old ways" and calling out these far-to-long accepted practices as bull shit. I challenge you to think of ways that we can make this better, I challenge you to not accept the status quo, and I challenge you to do a better job of supporting our professional family. Be that shoulder to cry on, be the friend that they can call, and just be available.

Life is way too short to hate what you do for a living. The writer Annie Dillard famously said, "How we spend our days is, of course, how we spend our lives." We spend a massive portion of our lives at work. Most estimates suggest that we spend around 90,000 hours working within our lifetimes. That is a long time to be miserable; that is a long time to be depressed. Of course, our jobs have a huge impact on our quality of life. We need to invest some quality time into making our work lives better. We must demand that our employers focus on making our work lives better; we can no longer accept being the "black sheep" and outsiders of the organizations in which we work. We must insist that the professional organizations, the ones that we give millions upon millions of dollars to every year, start to look out for us and our wellbeing. That, or we should stop giving them millions of dollars every year just for some stupid card and a conference here and there. Investing in the health and wellbeing of safety practitioners would be a much better use of our time and money; a lot better than those dumb ass conferences anyway. No really, have you been to those shindigs? They suck. You are damn right I am mad; I hope you are mad too! I have seen us lose too many amazing people to other jobs or to the other side, just because we cannot treat people right. Good people gone, some forever, simply because we will not care for people the way that we should. That is bull shit, you know it, I know it, everyone knows, and it's time we work on it.

I am Mr. doom and gloom, I know! There are a lot of systematic and insidious problems that we need to work on; but we are officially "WOKE" now and I'm certain that we will tackle them. I am sure of it; I see a lot of amazing changes already taking place. Change is just slow, too slow really. But here is some good news: you'll figure out how to deal with and overcome some of these issues on your own. Some will self-resolve with experience, you will move on from employers that do not deserve to have you, and you will find some healthy coping strategies that you can employ. But, in the meantime, here are a few good ways that I have found to "grow through" the hard times. These are some things that you can use while we are fixing the setting in which we work:

Find a mentor – This is huge! I lucked up and had a few amazing mentors; these are folks I still call to this day. They act as a voice of reason, guiding me through the hard times. They let me vent and complain; they help guide me on how to deal with the issues many of us face in our careers.

Lean on family & friends – Do not shut them out, tell them what's going on; give them the opportunity to support you through challenging times. I tried really hard to be "tough" and "leave work at work!" That does not work so well when your phone is ringing at 2:00 AM. They see it already, open up and talk about it! Let them be there for you, so you can be there for them.

Disconnect – This is pro-tip #1: Nowadays, I work extremely hard to protect my personal phone number from work - if they get it, I change it. That sounds pretty harsh, but it's necessary. You need to draw a line. Here's pro-tip #2: Every day when I get home from work, I put my phone on airplane mode and put it in a kitchen drawer. I leave it there for a couple of hours each and every day. I go to the gym, I have dinner, I have quality family time and I just live my life without my work phone (and personal phone for that matter) for a few hours. It helps a lot more than you would think.

If I can leave you with a "To-Do" list, this would be it:

- Separate work and home as much as you can
- Take a few hours every day to disconnect
- Find people that you can lean on and lean on them

Those three things will not solve everything, but they help, and they help a lot.

When we make work better, we make our lives better. Simply put, by Making the World a Better Place to Work we make the world a better place all together.

If you are struggling and do not know what to do; reach out to a trusted friend or call the National Suicide Prevention Lifeline at 1-800-273-8255.

Some More Bull Shit

I have covered a lot of bull shit and I think I have really honed in on a pretty decent "hit list." I believe I have formulated a mostly inclusive compilation of the challenges that the average safety professional faces. This compilation has been based off my own experiences and the experiences of others that I have witnessed firsthand. I will never be able to dream up every situation one could possibly face; there is no way I could predict every nuanced dilemma someone might find themselves in. Sure, we have talked about a lot of issues in this profession. We have not only called out quite a few of the problems, but we have also proposed some solutions. Let's level here, there are a lot of things that are problems out there. There are problems and issues that are simply not quite long enough to warrant their own chapter. Even more problematic, some are too long to attempt to squeeze into a small sliver of a book. Especially a book that I set out to make a "quick and fun read!" But these issues still need to be brought out into the open; we must still talk about them. Even if it is just a brief mention or quick thought; at least we can acknowledge their existence. I feel that I would be doing all of us a disservice, I would feel that I left this work unfinished, if I did not at least pull them out into the sunshine and touch on them. We must drag them from the darkness and into the light. The saying commonly attributed to former Supreme Court Justice Lewis Brandeis really does hold true; "Sunshine is the best disinfectant." Although his actual quote was a little more eloquent "If the broad light of day could be let in upon men's actions, it would purify them as the sun disinfects." Bad ideas fester in darkness; they are perpetuated and become "those that we do not speak of!" We must first pull them out into the light and we must then pick them apart; that is exactly what I am going to do. Just so you know, this will be a "rapid-fire" round. I will be noticeably more brash for time's sake; I will be quick and aggressive. But, even with that, I hope to give you quantity and quality. So, lets jump right in.

Professional Societies – There are only a couple of professional organizations that are out there; ones that actually count at least. They host a few boring conferences each year, throw together some crappy certificate programs, and pretend like they add value to our profession. They are "for-profit" organizations. I get that and I am perfectly fine with that, but wow! Have you seen what it costs to join? Have you seen what it costs to head to a conference? They provide B-rate bland and starchy courses and we shell out a grand to go. We then stand back and say "Oooh Ahhh, they had selfie stations and networking!" Give me a break. Year after year these

84

organizations continue to lose relevance. They are on a slow road to extinction. They need to adapt to the needs of the modern safety professional, they need to stop perpetuating all of the bull shit that we have discussed, and they need to actually focus on making the world a better place for safety people. If they do not, we need to stop giving them our cash.

Safety Professional Credentialing – Similar to professional societies, there are very few credentialing bodies. In all honesty, there is one or two at best. These certifying bodies appear to simply cram as much as they possibly can into their exams and perquisite requirements; making their certifications a little harder to get than some other things. Due to this they create prestige and can charge a premium price. My primary beef here is not really with them; I actually think they do a decent job for what they are up against. I just find that credentials do not mean very much in the real world. I will pick on the practitioners here; we have all seen it. When you see it on social media, for some reason, it makes it that much more hilarious: John Doe, FRT, CCC, MVC, GHH, GGG, TRE, LOP, QWE, SAFE, GHG-I, GHG-II, GHG-III, JJJ, GH, ASS. All it does for me is make me "LOL" at John Doe. We get it John Doe; you are a pompous ass.

Safety Professional Training and Continuing Education – There is a complete lack of quality courses for safety professionals. From initial courses to continuing education, we have continued to rely on the same old dry and boring B.S. classes. I can hear an instructor now "Can anyone tell me what year OSHA was founded?" While I pin some of this on our "most sacred" professional organizations; it is not all their fault. Most of us need those credits to maintain all of those fancy letters after our names. You know, the ones from those fancy credentialing bodies. We need those dry and boring B.S courses! We keep paying their bills, why would they change a thing? We need to get off of this "put you to sleep" safety training, It's garbage. All that we continue to train safety professionals in is compliance this and that, filling chairs in OSHA class after OSHA class. We need to focus on soft skills, we need to teach professionals how to seek learning, and how to think about safety. We need to introduce new and fresh perspectives around safety, we need to basically do anything else, rather than recycling the same old same old. We do not need to just teach safety pros what the rule book says, we need to teach them how to think. We need to demand better and we need to create better.

The "Jack of all trades" mindset – This fits in with the know-it-all chapter; I know, I know! But here, I want to call us out on the carpet. We like to think that we can handle it all; that we are a jack-of-all-trades. Look, it is good to have a broad knowledge base; to be a decent safety professional you should probably have a broad knowledge base. I am not arguing against that at all. What I am saying is this; do not get so focused on knowing everything that you end up knowing nothing. Find you niche and zero in on it. I am "The HOP Nerd," but I'm still "Safety Sam." I know a little bit of this and a little bit of that, but human & organizational performance is my thing. I lean on friends and peers; I lean on subject matter experts for the rest of what I need to know. Find your niche, build your peer group, and do not think for a moment that you should know everything.

Safety Cops – Take off the shiny badge and put down the baton; step away from trying to be a cop. Some do this because they like power, but I honestly think that most people do this because it's easy. One simply needs to know the rules and go out and enforce the rules; no need to think about context or anything else for that matter. Simply cite the rules out of your ass and demand compliance; compliance or else that is. The harder part of this is that many organizations and leaders of organization see this as beneficial; often praising and rewarding the safety cop approach. It fits their simplistic view of work; we have all heard it "if they just follow the rules than everything will be fine!" Being a safety cop is bull shit and you should not do it; this approach only harms and it never helps. If this sounds familiar to your approach, please stop doing this. If you cannot stop, get the hell away from this profession.

Mixing safety and human resources – Wait, someone thought this would be a good idea? Well, it's a pretty terrible idea actually. Hey, I really love our HR family (no,

I really do. Shut up! I am not just saying that so they will not fire me). But HR and safety have no business being in business together; they should be on different planets as far as I am concerned. Let's play a quick game! It is called "should we mix safety and HR?" Are you ready? Ok, here we go! Would you like to totally shut down event reporting? Would you really love to completely stop learning? Do you want everyone to run away in fear of discipline every time a safety professional walks out on the floor? Do you want an HR person with zero knowledge of occupational safety and health to make safety decisions for your organization and oversee your safety practitioners? Yes? Great! Mixing safety and HR it is, enjoy destroying your workforce and degrading your company's morale! I know, I know, I am being a little over dramatic. But really, it never ends well. We have our own image problems to overcome without mixing in HR's. At some point in history someone decided that we were similar enough of professions to just mix; two jobs one hire! It was probably some head-up-their-ass executive that that thought they could pinch a few pennies and pull a bigger bonus. I lightly scratched the surface on issues, there are a lot more. To keep this simple, lets just say nope, never, no, nae, not on your life, no siree, negative, by no means, not under any circumstances, absolutely not, nah, and hell no. You should never mix safety and HR!

Seagull safety people – For those that are not quite sure what "seagull safety" is, let me explain. Seagull safety is a technical term describing the interaction between a not-so-great safety professional and an induvial or group of individuals (commonly referred to as a "crew"). Seagull safety occurs when the safety professional "flies over" a job, shitting on (pointing out wrongdoings or imperfections) the work and then flies off, offering no real input or solution to those involved. Obviously, this one is mostly on us. But organizations have reduced many of their safety roles to an "observe and report" style of interaction. Companies send safety professionals on this wild adventure to complete observations and trend them; we have become glorified data collectors in some cases. So, it is not completely on us. Either way, its existence hinders us from having meaningful interactions with employees and prevents us from learning how work normally occurs.

Collegiate safety programs – We do not do a very good job of preparing young and green safety professionals for this job; we beat that topic to death early on. To target collegiate EH&S programs in a little more detail; new safety candidates leave college prepared to be compliance professionals. Most EH&S programs have distilled this profession down to practitioners being rule interpreters and rule enforcers. Students leave with a great understanding of regulations, rules, and law and they end up failing as safety practitioners. In addition to that, much of the safety management styles and techniques that they continue to teach are based off dated, flawed, and disproven techniques. We need to do better; we must do better. Look, there are some great colleges out there, some that are cultivating great safety practitioners. I am by no means lumping everyone together here, but let's just face it. Most college level EH&S programs suck.

With all of that being said, we really have covered a lot, huh? With the close of this chapter, I have hopefully curated a list of most of what ails you. If I have missed something (which I know that I have) please send it to me. If you have stories that you would like to share, I would love to hear them. No, really, send them to me! Send me an email to safetysucksbook@gmail.com. We need to continue to seek and destroy the not-so-great parts of what we do. We need to continue this conversation; we must not allow this work to get cold or become stale. I really believe that through these conversations we can make the world a better place to work. When we encounter bull shit we must first acknowledge it for what it is, we must talk about it, and then we must do something about it. So this is not a compilation of complaints; this is a book of actions.

In the Year 3000

We have spent quite a bit of time together by now; we have talked about a lot of stuff. I hope that my words have resonated with you. I hope that it has struck a nerve, I hope that it has made you angry, I hope that it has opened your eyes to the fact that you are not alone, but most of all, I hope that it has inspired you. The future of our profession is only as bright as we make it. Let me pull that apart a bit before we go any further; that is a strong "WE." We must do this thing together. Look, I get it. There are people in our field that will never come around; they will cling to the old ways forever. They will be screaming "but that's the way we have always done it!" with their last breath as the ship sinks to the abyss. There are companies that will always be horrible to work for, no matter what your chosen profession. There will always be god awful leaders and mangers; people that constantly try to devalue safety as a profession. But I do not believe for a moment that those people or companies are the majority. There are so many great and amazing people in this profession; there are so many great and amazing people in our industries. We have so many diverse, caring and innovative people, all that are "WOKE" to the B.S. within our line of work. All, having

91

the same or similar mission to – Make the World a Better Place to Work. These people are driven, they are passionate, and they are hungry for change. We will disagree and we will have different and varied approaches. We will all hold unique views as to how we can best bring about change. Those disagreements, those different opinions, and those unique views are exactly what we need. Our diversity makes us smarter; our diversity makes us stronger.   I have tried to make it a point to state this several times; I am not a guru! I speak out actively against the guru archetype. I speak out actively against the know-it-all safety elitist crowd in general. I am just a simple guy, a safety professional, a HOP nerd, and an evangelist of betterment. I do not hold all the answers. Hell, I probably do not hold most! At best, I simply have keen observations skills, a few good ideas, and enough time to write some stuff down.   At the end of the day, I simply want to make the world a better place to work. If that happens via my ideas, cool. If that happens via your ideas, even better. But if that happen through OUR ideas? That is the magic sauce! We, together, will find the answers. Together we will learn and create real and lasting betterment for our profession, our companies, and our industries. We have a long and challenging road ahead of us, but together, we can accomplish anything.

It is pretty safe to say, since you have made it this far, you have found a pretty sizable portion of the examples and stories in this book relatable. That is pretty good for me, writing and publishing a book and all. But it is a terrible indicator for the state of the safety profession. It tells me that the ridiculous, wacky, wonky, and sometimes, downright awful things that we have discussed, are typical things that safety professionals face. It tells me that these experiences are pretty normal for a safety person to go through. How can we accept that? How can we allow that to continue? There is a really simple answer here; we shouldn't. We should not accept safety professionals being worked into the ground simply due to staffing and funding issues. We should not accept them being used, abused, and belittled by organizations and leaders that do not understand the function of a safety practitioner. It must not be ok for us to compromise our health and wellbeing to appease mangers and companies. We should not accept occupationally induced depression and anxiety as "normal" parts of our profession. What we should do is give the safety profession the same amount of dignity and inherent worth that is bestowed upon other professions. The ridiculous things that we face in this profession nearly caused me to walk away from it all together. There were many reasons to leave and never look back; but I am glad that I decided to stay. I have made it part of my mission to eliminate as many of those reasons as I can. I have watched this job lead to depression, I have seen it ruin marriages and relationships, and I have seen it cause amazing colleagues and friends to leave the profession and never return. Listen, I am not trying to be a complainer, I promise I am not. I have a lot to be grateful for; I have an amazing job and a very blessed life. I have had the opportunity to meet some of the most amazing people on this planet; many of which I am fortunate enough to be able to call friends. I have done good work, I have helped people, and I have left things better than I have found them. This job has brought me experience, knowledge and "knowhow" that I would have never known without it. I am proud of what I do. I am proud of this profession, even with all the B.S. I am not a victim; we are not victims. The future is within our control. We have a responsibility to create betterment. We have a duty to learn from the past, call out the bad, and take action to change it. We are not sitting around and complaining; hoping and praying that the world gets better for us. We are not simply yelling and screaming; demanding that others fix these problems for us (although a little help would be nice). The future is in our hands; we get to decide and help shape the future of this career. How does it all end up? I am not completely sure. But, one thing that I know, we have an obligation to leave this job better than how we found it. Let me take a dive into what I mean by better; let us take a quick jump into the future.

As I am laying there groggy and foggy, I can hear a persistent and nagging "bzzzzzzz, bzzzzzzz, bzzzzzzz" coming from the nearby nightstand. I flop and roll around, knocking over water bottles and pictures from the nightstand to retrieve the culprit. I wrestle with and attempt to tame this wretched beast; pressing every button that I can until it finally stops. Just as my head begins to sink back into the cozy cool pillow, I think to myself, "it's Thursday! I need to get to work!" You see, it is a big day at Imaginary XYZ Corp., we are brining in a new hire safety professional and we are having a planning meeting for an upcoming project. On top of that, we have been making some really great progress in the safety space. Imaginary XYZ Corp. has really become enlightened to more modern views on safety and health. It has been great for the company and for our employees. I am honestly pretty excited to get to work today. Another alarm on my phone begins to blare, it is like a starting pistol this time! I jump from the bed; this is the starting line for the "morning routine race" and I am off! From shaving, to the shower, and jumping into some clothes; I then race down the stairs and towards the coffee pot. I say under my breath "Coffee, keys, backpack" and think "ok, I am good to go." I shout up the stairs "love you all!" I am off to the garage and into the car; the next thing you know I am pulling into work. First things first, lets meet this new person. She was as amazing in person as she was during her interview; knowledgeable and smart. She has a good demeanor and is really genuine and caring to boot. I think that she will fit in well here with our group. We have really stepped up our game when it comes to finding and hiring safety practitioners. "I hate to say hello and run" I say. But continue to explain "I need to make the pre-project meeting. We can catch up after!" I am off yet again. The meeting was a pretty good experience overall; safety had a seat at the table, both figuratively and literally. We had an open and real dialog about staffing; we are getting a couple contract safety folks to help during the project. We had a long discussion about the importance of time-off and work/life balance for everyone involved with the project. With that being settled, I link back up with the new safety professional. We are off to a learning review; I really want her to see how we facilitate learning in the company. We left the learning review proud of what we had just been a part of. Several frontline employees proposed some great solutions to a problem that we had been experiencing; a couple of managers are now getting involved to help them make it happen. We really like to listen and learn from "those that do" around here. Pretty neat stuff, huh? I finally have some time towards the end of the day to outline the job and structure to the new safety person. I begin by explaining that our role here is to act as consultants and support the organization; that we are agents of betterment that focus on learning. I explain our clear and concise reporting structure and explain our expectations around time-off "we expect you to take time away from work. If you are feeling tired or need a mental health day, we fully expect you to take it. In fact, we insist on it! If you just need a day away, we expect you to take it." she nodded as I continued, "and when you are off, you are off! None of this being tied to your work phone stuff!" we both chuckled. "Also, we are flexible. If you need to work from home some days that's perfectly acceptable as well." We wrapped up and said our goodbyes to each other and the office, "afternoon everyone! I will see you all next week!" I have a little get away planned with the family; Friday has come early for me. And just as quickly as it started, my day was over. I get home, turn off my phones, and drop them in a kitchen drawer. It is time for what I live for; it is time for family time.

That sounds like a pretty good day, right? There will still be bad; there will still be times that are not as great. But those are now the abnormal, the out of the ordinary. Back to a previous point we made: "Work sucks, that is why they call it work." But nowadays, work sucks a whole lot less. I know that some of you reading this are thinking "Yeah right, what's with all of this utopian bull shit?" and my response to you is, really? Really? Waking up and being happy to go to work, because work is not awful, is "utopian?" Going to work and it not resulting in depression and anxiety is unrealistic for our profession? If these are the beliefs that you hold, you are really saying this profession has become so terrible, so acceptably terrible, that we should be ok with that. You are saying that we should just be ok with things being terrible for safety practitioners in general. Look, I understand that there is a huge element of personal things that go into some of this as well. Mindsets, personal beliefs, and personal values are all a big piece of this puzzle. But the setting matters, and the setting matters a lot. We must work on what we can, making the working environment better. So when I hear people say things like "Things might be terrible, but they

are our things! That is the way we have always done it!"
and my personal favorite "If you do not like it, leave!" I
can only chuckle at the ignorance of their comments. Just
listen to how dismissive they are. That sentiment
completely opposes the idea of betterment. I find it
personally hilarious; only because I would cry otherwise. It
is like hearing "Well, I didn't ask to be born" from an
unruly child. It is just a strategy for avoiding the work it
will take to correct the problem, rather than accepting the
problem exists and working on it. I am big fan of using the
generic adoption curb. If you do not know what that is, I
encourage you to put this book down right now and go look
it up. Understanding and using it will help you
tremendously in your work. We will have laggards; people
that are slow to change. Some of these people will actively
rally against positive changes in our profession. Some will
do this out of spite; many will simply cling to tradition for
traditions sake. I am not here to argue with them, as they
have every right to their beliefs. The way I believe we
move forward, even against opposition, is by talking about
better ideas. We mentioned that very early on; we move
beyond bad ideas by introducing better ideas.

That is ultimately how we create the betterment that we
seek; we continue to introduce better and better ideas. So,
when people ask me "how can I help?" That is what I tell
them. Yes, we need to call out the bull shit that exists; of
course, the first step is to acknowledge the problem. But
we often freeze and stop there, never actually bettering

anything. We have the cathartic experience of cussing god and profession and then we simply go back about our lives. That is ultimately the challenge that I give you; the same challenge that I have posed multiple times in this book. Come up with better ways to do things! The good ideas will eventually outweigh the existing bad. I have proposed a few ways I believe that can be accomplished, but they are simply my opinions. They are simple and very reductive. It will take all of us, diving deep into problems and proposing better ideas, to bring about broad and sweeping change. We are an amazing, innovative, and diverse group of professionals and we must capitalize on that. Between all of us, it will be amazing to see what this profession looks like in the coming years. This is simply problem identification; this is just me calling bull shit, bull shit. This is a rallying-cry for betterment, a rallying-cry that I hope is heard and inspires betterment in our profession for years to come.

I am going to say something here that you probably are not expecting, but I like to end on a positive note. We have the best job in the world. Crazy, right? Let me explain. We have a job in which we can go out and make the world a better place for people to work. By making working lives better, we are making lives better overall. We can go out and influence companies and often complete industries to take better care of people. We have a profession that allows us to go out and be curious; learning from those that do "real" work. We get to help make lives better, we get to build relationships with great and diverse people, and all of that (and a lot more) is what makes this the best job in the world.   But it is time that we took a few moments to focus on makings things a little better for ourselves; we must set our own house in order.   We must "tend to our own wounds" before we continue working on everyone else's. It really boils down to this; It is about damn time that we made the world a better place to work for safety professionals, too.

Afterword

I hope that you have found value in this book, I hope that within its pages you have found unabridged honesty about the things that plague this profession, and I hope that you found it to be relatable and enjoyable. But most of all, I hope that it has inspired you to go out and seek betterment. We do not have any excuses to allow our beloved profession to remain in the state that we currently find it. We have a responsibility; we have a duty to go out and Make the World a Better Place to Work. We have a duty to make the world a better place to work for us as well. For far too long we have neglected our own wellbeing, all the while caring for everyone else's. It is time that we learn and grow; we must push away from "the way that we have always done things." I really hope that you take the ideas that were presented here and run with them, I hope that you add to them and come up with your own innovative solutions. I hope that you find other areas that we must make better and I hope you go out and change the world.

It was not that long ago that I wrote a brief article entitled "The 6 Sucks of Working in the Safety Profession:

The bull shit that they don't tell you about." I quickly realized that I had struck a nerve within the safety community; it has been one of my more popular articles to date. I remember posting it and not thinking very much about it; it was just another article. I do my best to just focus on truth telling; pouring out my observations onto the paper. I had simply done just that, writing an article addressing some things that had been on my mind for a while about the profession. I had lashed out at the things in the safety profession that should change, the things that hurt our safety practitioners. Overnight I received email after email and my social media accounts received numerous messages. People were sharing their stories of the "suck" that they had encountered while doing this job. I read some that made me laugh so hard my sides hurt; others made me cry. I read stories of depression and anxiety, I read stories of burnout, I read stories of fear and retaliation, and I read stories of amazing people just trying to make things better in a broken system. Stories of people working to make the world a better place in a world that has been rigged against them. Story after story, I realized that this was much bigger than I initially thought. I came to the realization that something must be done.

I will level with you, the thought of writing a book had come up in the past; I have had several peers encourage me to write something. I always would quickly rebuff their ideas, "I am a HOP nerd, not a HOP author." I guess that still holds true; I ended up writing a book about the safety profession. Either way, even after the initial success of the article, I never really intended on writing a book. To be totally honest, while initially writing "The 6 Sucks of Safety" the thought did cross my mind. The material just gushed out onto the paper; the writing of that article was effortless and enjoyable. I thought to myself "this could be a book!" followed by a quick "Nah, too busy! Maybe I will write a follow up article." My life is a whirlwind; it is chaotic and messy. I am not complaining, I quite like it that way. Busy, chaotic, and on the go, brings me happiness. I just never really thought I would have the time to put pen to paper (fingers to keys is more honest I guess). But in the spring of 2020, we were hit with the COVID-19 pandemic, crippling the world and thrusting the entire country into lock down. My calendar had suddenly cleared up; my beloved chaotic and busy life was no more. I decided that It was time to start jotting down some ideas for the second article, a few minutes of writing turned into a few hours of writing. Those few hours turned into days and then weeks. I was writing "Safety Sucks!" before I even realized it. Thankfully I didn't realize I was writing a book or I would have talked myself out of it once again! Before I knew it, I had a first draft and then I had 5 drafts, and then I was off to print. It was one massive whirlwind of "GSD" (getting shit done, remember)? Now that I look back, I guess I was creating that busy and chaotic life I was so missing. Nevertheless, it seemed like it was completed in no time at all.

The "how" is usually pretty interesting; but it is not nearly as important as the "why." Some of my intent was to cover the things that I wish that someone would have told me about this job before I started; the stuff that I wish I knew. I wish I had known about the not-so-great things before I dove in head first, not so I could avoid the profession, but so I could be prepared for the profession. As you know by now, being unprepared for the "tough stuff" of this career nearly made me leave it all behind. I am not special; my case was not unique. Many amazing safety professionals enter this field blind to what awaits them. They are grossly underprepared for the bull shit that awaits. Sadly, many do not survive it; they often leave to pursue careers in other fields all together. Others tough it out and spend their entire careers dealing with abuse, depression, anxiety and other trademark calling cards of the bull shit within this job.

So, the remainder of my "why" was for this to be a rallying cry for change. This was meant to be a call to action for every likeminded safety professional to create betterment; to seek out the bad and fix it. For us to collectively zero in on the problems and issues that continue to ail this profession, to point them out, to call bull shit, to drag them out kicking and screaming into the daylight, pick them apart, and start a conversation about how can fix them. I truly hope that it does just that.

Also, I would love to hear your stories; I want to hear about the good, bad, and ugly that you have encountered in this job. Storytelling is important; it is obviously cathartic for us individually. But it is also important for our profession as a whole. It allows us a starting point for betterment and allows us to hone in on common or shared problems. You can send your stories to safetysucksbook@gmail.com Your anonymity will be respected, and I will not share your stories without your permission.

Thank you for spending some time with me and talking about the safety profession. The fact that you read this book means the absolute world to me. I really do believe that by having these conversations that we can make the world a better place to work. I know that together we can change the world. But it takes all of our collective "know-how" to make that happen; thank you for being a part of this. Thank you for joining us on this mission to create betterment. I want to say this one last time; I really love this job. I love it so much that I am done accepting the bull shit that has been introduced into it. I am tired of simply accepting things as bad. I know that you are tired of it too, now it is time that we do something about it. Now we go out on a mission to "seek and destroy" bullshit; we go out and make the world a better place to work for safety people, too. By making ours and others working lives better, we are making lives better, period. Making people's lives better sounds like a pretty good end goal to me. No more talk; let's go make the world a better place to work!

www.ingramcontent.com/pod-product-compliance
Lightning Source LLC
Chambersburg PA
CBHW021151090420
42740CB00008B/1038